with love,

Ellie

GOOD
GRIE F
LIVING THROUGH LOSS

BY
EMS
HANCOCK

Published by Ivy Network Books

Published by Ivy Network Books

97 Barlow Moor Road

Didsbury

Manchester

M20 2GP

info@ivymanchester.org

Edited by: Alistair Metcalfe

Proofing: Tim Pettingale

Cover Design & Art Direction by: Dan Hasler MESSAGE:CREATIVE

Graphic Design: Sam Bloomfield

First Edition. November 2013

ISBN: 978-0-9927271-0-9 (Hardcover)

eISBN: 978-0-9927271-1-6 (Kindle)

Scripture quotations marked NIV are taken from *The Holy Bible, New International Version (NIV)*. Copyright © 1973, 1978, 1984, 2011 by Biblica. All rights reserved.

Scripture quotations marked ESV are taken from *The Holy Bible, English Standard Version*. Copyright © 2001 by Crossway. Used by permission. All rights reserved.

Scripture quotations marked NKJV are taken from *The New King James Version*. Copyright © 1982 Thomas Nelson Inc. Used by permission.

Scripture quotations marked AMP are taken from the *Amplified Bible*. Copyright © 1954, 1958, 1962, 1964, 1965, 1987 by The Lockman Foundation. Used by permission.

Scripture quotations marked GNT are from the *Good News Translation in Today's English*. Copyright © 1992 by American Bible Society. Used by permission.

Scripture quotations marked NLT are taken from the *Holy Bible, New Living Translation*. Copyright © 1996, 2004, 2007. Used by permission of Tyndale House Publishers, Inc. All rights reserved.

Scripture quotations marked GWT are from *GOD'S WORD*, a copyrighted work of God's Word to the Nations. Used by permission.

DEDICATION

This book is dedicated to the Rookwood family.

'"The glory of this present house will be greater than the glory of the former house," says the Lord Almighty. "And in this place I will grant peace," declares the Lord Almighty." Haggai 2:9 (NIV)

Good Grief is written in memory of my lovely Mum, Carol Rookwood and my Grandma, Elaine MacFetridge who taught me the truth that death is dead and that Jesus is the ultimate Grief Thief!

WHAT PEOPLE ARE SAYING ABOUT GOOD GRIEF...

'Warm, accessible, feed-the-soul stuff. Ems mingles reality and inspiration – a wonderful combination. Highly recommended.'
Jeff Lucas (Author, Speaker and Broadcaster)
www.jefflucas.org

'The word "bereaved" comes from an old word meaning "robbed". All you have to do is live long enough and you will lose someone. It will feel like they didn't live long enough. Whether you are going through grief yourself or helping someone who is, you will need comfort way beyond words, which somehow this book provides.'
Anthony Delaney (Speaker, Author and Pastor of Ivy Manchester)
www.anthonydelaney.com

'*Good Grief* covers some of the most difficult seasons of life with light, humour and hope. For anyone who has ever lost someone, been disappointed by life or struggled to believe in God, this is a brilliantly communicated must-read.'
Andy Hawthorne OBE, (CEO, The Message Trust)
www.message.org.uk

'Ems Hancock has the perspective of a poet, the mind of a philosopher, and the heart of an angel. I can think of no one better to be our personal tour guide into the recesses and sunlit pathways of a life lived in truth and beauty, with a bit of wry humour sprinkled on. Follow her in these pages. You will be glad you did.'
Bob Hamp (Author of 'Think Differently, Live Differently', Executive Pastor of Pastoral Care Gateway Church, Southlake, Texas, and Licensed Marriage and Family Therapist)
www.bobhamp.com/blog/

'Ems is a very gifted writer and the subject matter of this book has affected us all. I have observed how she has experienced grief over the last few years and feel that this book deals with real feelings in an open and occasionally shockingly honest way, rather than what the text books tell us it should be. I have found this book very helpful in my own grief journey and highly commend it to you.'
Debra Green OBE (National Director, Redeeming Our Communities)
www.roc.uk.com

'At times beautiful, often funny, continually moving and searingly honest throughout, Ems reminds us that mourning makes our humanity more meaningful.'
Russell Rook (CEO, Chapel St)
www.chapelst.org

'Bereavement paths have comparisons and differences for every individual. In a society where faith often takes a back seat in this process, it is refreshing to read the journey of loss through the eyes of someone who has a strong bond with God and how this friendship creates its own elements of support and turmoil through this part of life's journey.'
David Gresty (Funeral Director Dip.FD, MBIE, LMBIFD and Editor, British Institute of Funeral Directors Journal)
www.agresty.com

'It's not often you come across such honesty and insight. If you are grieving over any sort of loss in your life, you must find a quiet space to read this book.'
Mike Ledger (Project Manager, IBM and Elder at Ivy Manchester)
www.ivymanchester.org

'It can be a cliché to say that something you read makes you both laugh and cry, but Ems' honest and helpful book had me doing both in the first few chapters. If you are looking for a "Ten steps to feeling awesome" self-help book, this isn't it. If you want something painfully and beautifully real, then you will find it here. You will find page after page of Hope. A senseless and reckless Hope. A Hope that believes that God makes all things new. Hope to believe that even grief can become good.'
Ian Henderson (Founder of The Naked Truth Project)
www.nakedtruthproject.com

CONTENTS

ACKNOWLEDGEMENTS

I could not have written this book without my best friend Jon, my amazing husband who has walked with me through the roughest (as well as the most beautiful) years of my life. I praise God for you! Thanks for all your help and encouragement with this, and all the many crazy projects I come up with before breakfast. I love you. XOXO

I also want to thank Ian and Jen Henderson for their love and constant support this year – and every year for a very long time. You guys are my Jesus family!

I am also really grateful to a new but good friend, Alistair Metcalfe, for all his hard work – editing, questioning and challenging me to help make this book what it has become.

Thanks to Tim Pettingale for starting me off as a writer and for telling me to 'Go for it!' with this little baby. Thank you too for proofing the final manuscript. I owe you a LOT of marmalade fella!

Thanks to Dan Hasler and all at Message Creative for an amazing product and for being so flippin' lovely and fun to work with.

All my beautiful pals who have helped me care for Esther during the writing weeks – Jo Spurling, Hannah Lamberth, Hannah Lodge, Shula Odell, Lucy West, Sian Ashford and Helen Firth. You are all so precious to me.

Our incredible Grow Group for many prayers and encouragements this year.

The One Café in Cheadle for allowing me to write there and drink lots of hot milk.

Ivy Manchester for being such an inspiring church family full of big thinkers and big huggers.

Westwood Christian Centre for the many wonderful retreats and writing sessions I have had there.

All the wonderful contributors to this book – those who are named and those who are not. I am so grateful you have let me tell your stories.

All those kind enough to say lovely things about the book and about me.

And finally, thank you to my darling family – my wonderful children, my brothers and my Daddy. I hope this book in some way blesses you to read as much as it has helped me to write.

PREFACE

'Light bulb!'

Gru (Despicable Me)[1]

I am a strange lady.

Even those who love me very dearly would agree that I can't be easily labelled. I don't have a job – although I have many pastimes. I don't currently have a specific role, unless you count wife and mother (which I never remember to do). I am a lot of things to a lot of people.

But, among other passions, one of the things I do is write.

I sometimes help people form their own books but I have rarely wanted to birth a whole tome myself. As a ghost writer, I know what kind of sacrifice and self-belief it takes, and I have often found myself – especially in this season of my life – woefully short of both.

However, throughout my experiences and circumstances over the last few months there has been both a nagging whisper in my heart and a tugging sensation in my spirit. Occasionally on the wind of my prayers there has been the breath of the words, 'Write it down! Write it down!'

In those moments, I have reached for my phone or my journal and scribbled furiously. Self-help, I guess.

I did not want to write a book this year. To be entirely truthful, I fought the very thought of it. Selfishly, what I most wanted was to discover a book that would help me through my grieving process – one that encapsulated the bizarre twists of emotions and aching fears that grief brings.

I wanted to read a book that I could relate to and that would give me some biblical anchors to hold on to. I only realised quite late in the proceedings that I was meant to write that book.

Oh.

But the fact that you are reading this is testament to the beautiful truth that God often has other plans for us. Much better plans too.

> 'Grief does not change you. It reveals you.'
>
> John Green[2]

This book was not primarily designed for you. Sorry about that, but I am just saying it like it is. I wrote it mainly because I needed to. I didn't even really think about getting it published, or showing it to anyone. But then, on retreat one day, God made it very clear that my little musings were not a self-help manual for me alone, but for others to cry and laugh over too. (I pray you do both.)

Then, a close friend of mine, who did not know I was collecting my thoughts on grief, had a word for me. In a text, she said: 'During my sleep I had a dream about you. We were in some sort of stock cupboard at church and there was a big box full of your book... one you had written as main author, not for someone else. Seemed like some sort of self-help book as some of them were packed up in bag/packet type things and I noticed they had a journal/notebook to use.'

Pretty clear confirmation, I'd say.

I have no pretensions about myself. I am not a theologian or a psychiatrist, a counsellor or a doctor. I don't have a degree in philosophy or any clever-schmlever stuff like that. But I felt very strongly that this shouldn't stop me obeying the call of God to write something... simple though it certainly is.

I hope, that, like a mum, or a big sister, or an auntie, I am going to just share some home truths with you in such a way that grabs you, comforts you and challenges you in the season of your soul right now.

My 'inheritance word' – as writer and speaker Graham Cooke terms it – is Isaiah 61. I take this passage very seriously because I feel it is my life call. It says, in the Amplified version:

'The Spirit of the Lord God is upon me, because the Lord has anointed *and* qualified me to preach the Gospel *of* good tidings to the meek, the poor, *and* afflicted; He has sent me to bind up *and* heal the brokenhearted, to proclaim liberty to the [physical and spiritual] captives and the opening of the prison *and* of the eyes to those who are bound...' (v. 1).

I love the fact that it says, 'anointed *and* qualified.'

That is my CV right there.

I take great comfort from that.

Isaiah 61 goes on:

'To proclaim the acceptable year of the Lord [the year of His favour] and the day of vengeance of our God, to comfort all who mourn,

'To grant [consolation and joy] to those who mourn in Zion—to give them an ornament (a garland or diadem) of beauty instead of ashes, the oil of joy instead of mourning, the garment [expressive] of praise instead of a heavy, burdened, *and* failing spirit—that they may be called oaks of righteousness [lofty, strong, and magnificent, distinguished for uprightness, justice, and right standing with God], the planting of the Lord, that He may be glorified' (vv. 2–3)[3]

> 'Grief can be a burden, but also an anchor. You get used to the weight, how it holds you in place.'
>
> Sarah Dessen[4]

Before you start to read any of this and before I put anything more on paper, I want us to understand each other.

I am not writing this as someone who has had time to process all the effects of the grief I am going through, but as someone still grieving. Therefore what you read may be a bit raw or unfinished in places. I am sorry if that's not very satisfying or comfortable for you.

I am aware that I may come across at times like the intense, crying girl on the stairs at a party... you know the one? The person who rambles on inconsolably, making deep sweeping, dramatic comments with little sense or structure and who everyone hopes will go home early with a headache?

Anyway, I am a bit like her, only hopefully a tad less annoying.

My pain in grief has been, and is still, very real. But I am definitely coming through it. It is not sanitised and wrapped up with a neat, sparkly bow. I am a work in progress.

This means that I may not speak at all times in this book with a nice happy 'everything is brilliant' Christian voice. Because that would be disingenuous, pointless, and unhelpful.

I want you to journey with me. This may mean travelling to new or familiar places in grief or disappointment. Parts of that journey aren't all that pretty, I can assure you. I am not always proud of my reactions and feelings over the past few months, my doubts and my fears. But I won't lie to you and say I haven't had them, because then this book would be as much use to you, and as dangerous for you, as an ejector seat in a helicopter.

And I would hate that. Because I wrote this to be useful and helpful and provoking and funny and, well, lots of things. Like I said, I am the girl on the stairs. And you are listening to me. I don't know if that's your fault or mine. But here we are!

> 'God has not been trying an experiment on my faith or love in order to find out their quality. He knew it already. It was I who didn't. In this trial He makes us occupy the dock, the witness box, and the bench all at once. He always knew that my temple was a house of cards. His only way of making me realise the fact was to knock it down.'
>
> C.S. Lewis[5]

God has used this time in my life to teach me what I am made of like no other.

Grief is no respecter of persons. But I am. So I don't want to offend you or make you want to speed-skate off and dial a hotline to my pastor.

My life is held in the grip and grace of God and I am going nowhere except nearer to him and his plan for me. But I have had my battles with him this year and this book shares some of the most poignant.

With that in mind, I offer the rawness of my emotions and feelings, the inadequacies of my answers and responses, just as they are.

So 'help yourself!' as they say.

But so much more than that – may God help you too.

And now, in the wise words of Lewis Caroll in *Alice's Adventures in Wonderland*, I will '... go on till I come to the end: then stop.'[6]

Ems Hancock, May 2013

DARK CLOUDS

WHEN GRIEF HIT ME

> 'If you have ever lost someone very important to you,
> then you already know how it feels, and if you haven't,
> you cannot possibly imagine it.'
>
> Lemony Snicket[1]

TAKEN

I woke up with a start. It was 6am. Jon was kneeling by the bed and leaning over me, looking pale and concerned. I knew something awful had happened.

'Ems, we have been robbed!' he said, quietly, so as not to wake the children.

'Oh no! What's gone?' I said.

'The laptop, Jamie's iMac and some phones. I don't know what else.'

I ran downstairs with him, my mind racing and my fears growing. As I saw the signs of the burglary – open drawers, my handbag contents spilt out onto the table – I suddenly felt sick. The thought of someone creeping around our house whilst we were all sleeping was hideous. Even if he was wearing gloves.

'It's metal and money,' I said. 'That's all.'

I was right. It could have been a good deal worse.

But it isn't totally 'all.' It is the thoughts that accompany the loss that you have to handle; the children's questions; the sleepless nights and the constant hearing of noises in the night. It is not just the total inconvenience of having to replace things, filling in the seemingly endless insurance forms, and 'going without' for a while, but the psychological effects of knowing your safety has been breached and your peace of mind has been eroded. Your world has been threatened, changed, altered... and all without your permission. Locks need changing. Alarms need fitting. Jewellery needs hiding. Lots of small and large adjustments occur mentally and physically.

For many people, grief feels like this – a robbery. It seems as though something, or more correctly, *someone*, who belonged to us has been taken. The vile violence of a death such as cancer can feel like a burglary, with GBH thrown in. A death of any kind without time to say goodbye can leave us feeling robbed not just of that person, but of many hopes and dreams. Being bereaved in whatever way can leave us with regrets and heartache that we fear may never fade.

Humanly speaking, death is often ugly. It is an assault on our emotions and our senses. It feels wrong to have no choice about something so powerful, overwhelming and consuming. People speak of it being unfair, unjust and unkind.

With good reason. This is how it feels. Often, anyway.

Death is THE RULES. It is the ultimate statistic: one in one die.

What if there was another way to see it? What if it wasn't always cruel, but merciful? What if it was part of a rich, incredibly intricate plan to restore us and put us back where we belong?

What if a person dying wasn't being taken away from where they belonged but taken back to where they would always belong?

What then?

BROUGHT HOME

For those of us who have the gift of faith, death can be a beginning and not just an end. It is still hard, horrid and painful for those 'left behind' (and we would be big fat liars to call it anything else) but it CAN also be hopeful, glorious and dignified.

We do not belong on earth. Our home is actually in heaven. So when we leave earth, we are not suddenly homeless, or staying at some crummy temporary B&B. We are actually going home. For the very first time.

ame is a place where you can truly be yourself. None of us can be that way on earth – not fully. Why? Because we do not have the constant and manifested presence of the ONE in whom we find all our belonging, meaning and destiny: GOD. His home is in heaven, too.

However gory, gruesome, terrifying, awkward, precious, painful, surprising, amazing, upsetting or noble our actual death is, our eternal destination, as believers, is the same and it is secure.

Matthew Henry, the famous scholar and Bible commentator, was once accosted by thieves and robbed of his money bag. Afterward, he wrote these amazing words in his diary: 'Let me be thankful first, because I was never robbed before; second, because, although they took my purse, they did not take my life; third, because, although they took my all, it was not much; and fourth, because it was I who was robbed, not I who robbed.'[2]

I find this perspective fascinating. Henry had gone through the trauma of robbery, like many others before and after him, and yet this lovely man chose to see it differently. He was able to see the hand, mercy and grace of God in it all.

I am learning, albeit in the manner of a slow boat to China via Chingford, that God is STILL good in this season of my personal grief. As a friend said at a prayer meeting recently, God has a 100% track record: GOOD! GOOD! GOOD! Not only is he always good, he is always abundantly and unstintingly kind.

Second Corinthians 1:3–4 says:

> 'Blessed be the God and Father of our Lord Jesus Christ, the Father of mercies and God of all comfort, who comforts us in all our affliction, so that we may be able to comfort those who are in any affliction, with the comfort with which we ourselves are comforted by God' (ESV).

God can comfort us. He is able to.
God wants to comfort us. He is longing to.
God will comfort us. He has promised to.

Let me take you back a bit... to where my grief began.

Finding out the extent of my Mum's cancer was devastating. It made me ask a whole load of questions of myself, and God, that I had never needed to face before.

What was my faith built on?

Was it strong enough to withstand the pressure of this awful situation?

Would God heal Mum and be glorified through that?

What if he didn't?

I have been through enough shadows to learn how to cling to God in darkness. I have been through enough valleys to know how to keep walking, even when everything around me looked bleak, black or blessing-free. But I had never seen anyone I loved live with the knowledge that they were going to die. That was new.

My own Mum was dying. And it wasn't nice.
In fact, it felt evil.

So how did death get into our world in the first place? Surely a loving God would not ever have designed something so awful as dying and death. Would he?

Here is my take on what happened all those years ago, back in the garden of Eden. It doesn't make for very comfortable reading (or writing). But I hope it helps you see it as it may have been...

They stood naked, shivering and awkward behind the biggest tree they could find, shamed and humiliated, not even daring to look at their own bodies, let alone one another's. Childlike acceptance was dead, and in its place stood barbed, throbbing regret. There was no going back now. Robbed of innocence, even the very ground had seemed to sting and bite them as they ran to hide.

Eve stood defiant, her eyes full of blame. Adam couldn't bear to even look at her, wanting the 'flesh of his flesh' to leave him alone to clear his head and work out what he would say.

Then they heard the terrible sound of God walking in the garden. It had never been terrible before. It had made them run towards him, scampering playfully, knowing deep, shared joy and fun was on the horizon; peaceful communion; family; friendship; love. But that was then. What had they done? One piece of fruit did all this?

Knowledge of evil filled every pore, every fibre and sinew. They knew evil thoughts, feelings and desires for the first time; thoughts, feelings and desires that began to rot the purity of the divine out of them. They felt it bleeding away, leaking loving trust and withering their spirits as it left. Gaping holes where once comforting friendship with God had been, began to gnaw into their souls.

God called to them. They held their breath, hoping He would pass by. But he called again:

'Where are you, my children?'

Neither answered. Adam looked fearfully at the ground, digging the unfamiliarly hard earth with his toe. Eve tossed back her hair, angry that she felt to blame and reaching into her newly-tainted mind for someone else to throw it upon.

Everything in her screamed out, 'It's not my fault. I was tricked!' A sudden lurching pain gripped her deep in her stomach and made her open her mouth in agony.

God stood still, his wonderful creative breath hanging limp in the dark silence as he turned to face them.

'Why are you hiding?' he said, his voice slow, deliberate and pungent with sadness. He knew that sin was present and the weight of it was suffocating his heart.

'We... we have no clothes to cover our bodies,' they protested lamely.

'And who told you that you were naked?'

'We just.... knew.

Adam spoke, holding Eve to blame. Discord filled the air.

Eve's anger spattered out as the bullets of her mind let rip: 'It was the snake! He tricked me! Nothing to do with me!' Her tongue dripped the venom well.

God stared at his beloved children. They talked and acted like strangers. He read Eve's mind and he hated every image he could see. She stood looking back at him, haughty pride in her eyes.
'Come out,' said God eventually; words that his own Son would say to every evil spirit he encountered.

'Are you going to make me?' said Eve, in her heart.

And in His wounded heart God ached.

'I already did.'

The truth is that God planned us to have a very different kind of life. He planned us to only ever know life of the everlasting kind. But he knew he couldn't force us to accept the truth that he is God (and that, therefore, we are not) without some kind of lesson. Hence the fruit tree.

We all think that if we had been there it would have been different, don't we? We would have seen the trap of that wily snake and been triumphantly naked forever, securing for all time the consummate failure of all fashion houses and the prosperity of nudist holiday camps everywhere. Yay for us!

But that's tosh and we know it. The fact is, there is an Adam or Eve-like character in all of us. (I mean, I am tempted by every new Apple they bring out – love him or loath him, that Steve Jobs was a ruddy genius!)

Seriously. We would have messed it up too, wouldn't we?

Death came into the world. Not the death of a relationship with God. That did not die... at least not fully. It was death that meant that the word 'goodbye' came into our language. 'For as in Adam all die...' (1 Corinthians 15:22)

SAFE IN UNCERTAINTY
BY: EMS HANCOCK

BLOG
POST
MAY
12th
2012

Yesterday I was sitting in the car, singing my head off and truly smiling. You might think this is nothing unusual for me. Those of you who know me well understand that singing is a common part of my day. And yet my singing was from a different place in my spirit yesterday.

Three days ago, we found out that my Mum has liver cancer - and potential cancer elsewhere too. It is amazing how things like that change your priorities and reorganise your mind. It is amazing how your wallpaper doesn't seem quite so in need of urgent repair and your electric bill seems so much less significant.

I have found myself ordering my world and my thoughts very differently in these past few days - of being very clear what I want to take on and what I don't.

My parents are being incredibly brave and trusting in the circumstances - especially in these pre-test days of not knowing exactly what they are facing.

But together we are choosing to praise God in all things. We are finding it is possible to trust him fully in the uncertainty and despite the tears.

When I was singing yesterday I meant EVERY word. I was listening to the Israel Houghton song:

'You hold my world in Your hands,
You hold my world in Your hands,
I am amazed at Your love,
I am amazed that You love me...
My world is safe in Your hands...'[4]

I feel so safe, so cared for and so upheld. I know angels have been charged to watch over us and even though my role as one of the family anchors may be tested and tried in the coming days, I know that with God's help I will be able to bear all things and be found faithful.

These may be dark days, but I have a very bright God who I know is at work for His glory to be revealed. I know it will come…"

'WE
DON'T
SEE
THINGS
AS
THEY
ARE,
WE
SEE
THEM
AS
WE
ARE'

THE TALMUD

But what if death is not actually like burglary at all? What if it is not some kind of cosmic punishment, designed to leave us flailing, depressed and thoroughly miserable ad infinitum?

What if death was God's way of transporting us to that place again? To Eden? I put it to you that God designed death to take us to him and put us right with him forever. If I am right, death is not loss, but gain.

It is not defeat, but victory.
It is not miserable, but glorious.
It is not a journey to the other side, but a journey to the ONLY side.

I think this is how my Mum came to view it anyway.

In the days before she died she showed real courage and even humour. Her email updates to praying friends showed the lightness of her spirit. This is an extract from an email she sent after her biopsy from one of the cancers on her head:

> 'I was shown into a private room with en-suite loo. The nurse gave me one of those fetching one-size-fits-nobody hospital gowns, which was to fasten at the back, and (never had this before) also a dressing-gown, which fastened at the front. So I was decently covered for my walk through various areas to the theatre. There she handed me over to a young man named Mark, wearing theatre scrubs and attractive J-cloth headgear, who dealt with the consent form. He told me the theatre team was ready for me. I was a bit puzzled.
>
> Me: So, Mark, what is your function here?
>
> Mark: To keep talking to you during a rather unpleasant procedure and distract your mind from what's going on.
>
> Me: Oh, good. Do you tell jokes?
>
> Mark: No – I can never remember the punch lines.
>
> Me: Well, that's not much use. Do you do song-and-dance?

Mark: No, just conversation.

We went into the theatre, surgeon plus four ladies, who were all introduced, as I was, by Christian names. The surgeon explained what he was going to do.

Surgeon: First you will feel a sharp scratch.

Me: Why do you medical people always say that, when what you mean is, 'I am going to stick a needle into you until it comes out at the other side'?

Surgeon: I'll do my best not to hurt.

Pause. Scrabbling behind me.

Surgeon: How was that?

Me: How was what?

Mark: That's the worst bit over.

Me: Well, in that case, you can start your stand-up routine now.'

Does this sound to you like a woman who is scared to die? Not really.

'We all have to die of something,' she would say.

She was calm, serene and full of hope and faith. As a family we were so blessed by her attitude. I know that it is a rare one to hold – even for someone who professes to be a Christian.

She made it easy for us. There was no 'why me?' Not one ounce of self-pity and never a single reproach or regret mentioned. She had lived well and she knew it. Now it was time to die well, too.

Each day, despite being constantly sick, not being able to hold down water or her many tablets, she still faithfully reached for her Bible to do her 'quiet time', just as she had done every day of her adult Christian life.

She was unafraid. And full of purpose.

But part of me was SO scared of her dying. I was scared of what it would mean for us as a family and scared of what it would do to my heart. I am a very strong woman but I was worried for myself, my dad and my brothers. As the Talmud says, 'We don't see things as they are, we see them as we are.' We can't help it.[3]

"I AM" IS HERE
BY: EMS HANCOCK

BLOG
POST
JUNE
8th
2012

I have not blogged for a bit... As many of you will realise, caring for someone with terminal cancer is far from a walk in the park.

It is often a bewildering fog: Who do I call? Who do I ask? What services are available? How can I stop this pain? Where can I get a hospital bed? What can I give her to eat? How many visitors can she handle? How is Dad coping? How are my brothers?

I have been shocked that there is so little information available (at least that I have been told about) on how to deal with the practical aspects of life right now... and I really praise God that He is the ROCK that stays solid and firm.

The family have been remarkable in terms of practical care. My sister-in-law-to-be for example sent me five large meals yesterday when my brother visited. I could have cried with the sense of relief that I can tick shopping off my lengthening to do list...

In fact, it is no longer a list - it is a book where I write down Mum's current medication, strength, frequency... her bank details and passwords, her funeral wishes, important numbers of who to contact (as and when I glean the salient information) building society details, friends who have visited and thank you notes that need sending.

I said to Jon yesterday that I feel as though someone has given me a new full time job that I didn't apply for and don't have the right experience for.

This is not what God says over me, however. This morning as I shared that little thought with him, he spoke gently over me words that Moses must have heard a number of times, 'Tell them I AM has sent you.'

There isn't much of a come back to that is there?

If God thinks I can, then I can. Not because of what I know and what I can do, but because of who HE is and what HE can do. If God thinks you can, you can!

So today, with God's help, leaning FULLY on Him, I am putting the CAN in CANCER.

And one day, perhaps I shall write a VERY HELPFUL book for families that helps them do the same.

God did not heal my Mum's cancer this side of heaven. Despite the many people praying and fasting for her, she died. She also did not live long enough to see my youngest brother get married –again, in spite of the many people praying and believing God for the contrary. She missed it by 12 days. I couldn't quite believe it. I still can't.

It was so sad.

I couldn't see the logic or reasoning of God behind it. I had begged him to let her stay alive long enough. It was her dearest wish. I had even booked a private ambulance and got one of the crew to come round so she could meet him and lie on the bed inside it to make sure it was suitable for her. She had also bought a beautiful Mother-of-the-Groom dress. But of course that was when she was nearly a stone healthier. Cancer ate away at her body like a ravenous wild animal, until the bones on her back stuck out like a dinosaur skeleton.

I couldn't bear to see Mum suffering. She never moaned once, although she was sick many times a day and unable to eat anything. She got worse every day.

One day a year ago now, God made the decision to 'promote her to glory' before I expected.

No amount of me not liking it was going to make a scrap of difference. He is the Boss and he works for good. So I had to trust it was right.

My brother's wedding was actually a totally amazing occasion. It felt like God was carrying us so wonderfully. Coming only six days after her funeral, we were all still reeling and exhausted but also so grateful that Mum was finally out of pain, restored and whole.

I led worship at the beautiful wedding service and we sang these words from the last verse of 'In Christ Alone' with a lump in all our throats:

No guilt in life, no fear in death,
This is the power of Christ in me;
From life's first cry to final breath.
Jesus commands my destiny.
No power of hell, no scheme of man,
Can ever pluck me from his hand;
Till he returns or calls me home,
Here in the power of Christ I'll stand.[5]

I meant those words like I have never meant them before or since. We all did.

Mummy was home.
Joel was married.
God was holding us.

A friend of ours uses an illustration that whenever we see a group photo we know we are in, we look for ourselves on it first. We just do. It is how we are wired. If we are not in the photo, we will look for our children or some other familiar face. Life is about how we feel about life. When we look for meaning, we start with ourselves and how we are feeling.

For months after Mum died, I would 'come to' in the morning and momentarily things would seem normal, but then the weight of the abominable truth SHE IS DEAD would dawn on me again. Tears would come and keep coming. Jon would look at me with worry and concern. Another day would begin in despair. I felt a long way from home with the sensation that someone had changed the locks.

'Every morning, I wake up and forget just for a second that it happened. But once my eyes open, it buries me like a landslide of sharp, sad rocks. Once my eyes open, I'm heavy, like there's too much gravity on my heart.'
Sarah Ockler[6]

ARRIVAL IN HEAVEN
BY: EMS HANCOCK

BLOG
POST
JUNE
20th
2012

As I write this I am indescribably tired and numb.

I cannot quite process the events of the last few days...

But on the 40th day after my Mummy was diagnosed with as many cancers as a human body can possibly hold, she was promoted to glory.

17th June, 2012, aged 68.

They say life begins at 40. Mum's certainly has!

I cannot explain how wonderfully peaceful and beautiful her death was. She left this earth, in my Dad's arms. A single tear (the only one she had cried to my knowledge) fell from her eye. My brother and his wife and my eldest brother were also there... so lovely to share this moment with them.

We had just sung to her a few songs from her childhood - and ours.

'Two little eyes to look to God...'
'Little boy kneels at the foot of the bed...'

I played her a song I had written that was her favourite of my creations.

I played her one of the arias in Handel's *Messiah*: *'I know that my Redeemer liveth'*

I can't really start to tell you anything about how I am feeling. There are such a jumble of thoughts and emotions - many of them conflicting...

But I have a few thoughts to offer:

1. Death is merely a horizon and a horizon is merely the limit of our sight. It is not a REAL line.
2. Whilst I cannot see my Mum anymore I have not LOST her. I know exactly where she is.
3. Also, she did not lose her fight with cancer (as so many often say). She has won the prize Christ set out for her.. and what a glorious one that would be!
4. She is united with Christ and the 'great cloud of witnesses' with him.
5. The BIG C is not Cancer. I have found it to be CHRIST. He is my all. He always has been and always will be SUFFICIENT for me.

May the Lord bless you and keep you and help you to know this for yourselves today.

I share this with you as I say goodbye to my darling Mummy.

NOT READY

First Thessalonians 4:13 is very clear that we do not grieve as those have no faith and the certainty of heaven. And this is so true:

> 'But we would not have you ignorant, brethren, concerning those who are asleep, that you may not grieve as others do who have no hope.'

I mean, we had not lost Mum in the sense that you misplace your keys and don't know where they are. Knowing Mum is safe, well, healed, happy, content, peaceful, reunited with loved ones, worshipping, praying, rejoicing and, no doubt, reorganising God's filing system, is a huge comfort.

But it doesn't bring her BACK.

She is not HERE.

I took a break from writing earlier today when I heard my daughter crying. She was ill today and woke up from her afternoon nap with a temperature. I held her close and said 'Mummy's here, darling. Mummy's here.' As I did so the tears rolled down my face. The thought that no one will ever say that to me, or be that for me EVER again (this side of heaven) is almost unbearable. I miss my Mum sometimes so much that I ache. If you have experienced grief recently I am sure you will know something similar.

> 'No one ever told me that grief felt so like fear.'
>
> C.S. Lewis[7]

After Mum died, a friend of mine had a dream about her which she wrote down and sent to me.

'I recall opening what appeared to be a back door and peering through and seeing you and your mum in what looked like a hot tub! You were sitting on the left and your mum on the right. You both had tears streaming down your faces. You did both speak to me, but I can't recall the short conversation. It looked like your mum had a video camera and that she was showing you something. Your mum then said something about dancing on the patio and singing, 'It's a wonderful life for me, it's a wonderful life'. She then got up out of the hot tub and started singing and dancing.

'At this point in the dream I had tears streaming down my face too – I can't recall now how I felt at that point in the dream. I then woke up and immediately looked at the clock, it was 6.20am.'

My friend did not really know the significance of that little vignette. But to me the dream's meaning was so clear: that Mum is having an amazing time in heaven, that she is no longer ill and feeble and unable to sing and dance!

The footage she was showing me was of all her friends in heaven (her Christmas card list was ridiculously extensive) in one mass choir praising God as she arrived!

Focusing on these feelings and comforting myself with the truths that I read in the Bible really feeds my soul and helps me not to dwell on my personal loss in an unhealthy way.

NOT STEADY

Of course, death doesn't just take away from you the person that has died but who that person helped others and you to be. That is one of the most profound things I have – and am still – coming to terms with.

You lose your 'place' in the world: everyone shifts up and you find your new space to be cold and unfamiliar to the touch, like an unwelcoming pew in a freezing church.

I was 39 when Mum died. I was not ready to be the matriarch of the family. When my Gran died a few months later, I truly felt the gaping hole of the female line. It was ME. Suddenly I was the eldest. At 40, that felt too young.

I have grown up with grandparents, their legacy and their friendship playing out in the minor and major details of my days. I wasn't just grieving the fact that I was going to miss out on precious years with my Mum, but that my children, or any children my brothers may have, would never have the kind of Grandma we had leant on all our lives. She just would not be there. Ever. That is not easy to get over. Or through.

GONE

In those few months following my Mum and my Gran dying, I experienced many physical signs and sensations of ageing. My hair suddenly went very grey. Then one day my hairdresser found that a whole section near my hairline had totally fallen out. I developed aches and pains everywhere and needed strenuous physiotherapy on my neck and shoulders. I was constantly cold and tired. I felt ten years older, but not ten years wiser. I lost confidence in many things I had once believed very strongly about myself. I looked in the mirror and wondered who was staring back.

In our lounge we have a large set of silver letters that spell out the word FAITH. I am a big believer in having words to cling on to, whatever is going on around me. At some point, during those few months, the children were playing with the letters and lost one of them. It was the letter ' I'.

The I of the word FAITH is the most important one. It is highly spiritually significant for me. On more than one occasion I have asked people I am praying with to take a literal hold of that letter – putting the 'I' of FAITH in their hands and expecting God's healing, blessing or change in their heart or situation.

Suddenly I had lost the 'I' of faith for myself. It felt like a parable of what was happening in my heart. I don't believe I ever lost my faith, but I lost a lot of hope. I was not sure what or why I was thinking the way I was, but I knew it was all very negative. A dark cloud seemed to follow me and the grey spirit of Eeyore took a deep root.

Friends tried to reach in and help me. But I felt alone. I felt as though no one truly understood the seismic shift that had happened in my world. I had lost ME. I had disappeared and I had no idea where to look for myself. I think I was very self- pitying. And the trouble with self pity is, it is a pit.

GOD LAY IN WAIT

I very rarely expect anything from anyone. On the whole I am very self-reliant. Some might say a little too much so. But for a number of days at my worst and lowest point, I felt very grumpy because none of the people I asked to pray for me were available at the exact second I felt I needed it. How dare they be busy! Some even suggested alternatives, but they wouldn't do! Oh, no.

I was feeling hurt, alone and upset – with God, with people and with me. I was totally disappointed in how my last eight months had turned out. And nobody was allowed in to my pity party. It was a solitary affair, with a lot of cake.

My long-suffering and wonderful Jon got a passage the following morning from Isaiah 59:16. It completely made sense to me as a word from God:

'He saw that there was no one, he was appalled that there was no one to intervene; so his own arm achieved salvation for [her],
and his own righteousness sustained [her]' (NIV).

I asked Jon if I could book myself some time away to be by myself and see if God could work some kind of miracle in my heart. He was delighted to make it happen and bent over backwards to take a couple of days off work to ensure I could go to my favourite retreat centre and not worry about childcare for our four little people.

On the journey there I begged God to meet with me, beseeching Him for a change in my spirit. I had had enough. I had wondered if I had been facing some kind of awful life-sapping depression but had dismissed it. 'I am not that type of person,' I thought. 'Anyone who had been through what I had would feel sad. It's all circumstantial,' I reasoned.

(Don't get me wrong, I am not saying there is no such thing as depression or that it is 'all in your head'. I totally believe that clinical depression exists and that it is a medical and treatable illness. I just did not think that I was in that category. More than this, I hoped and prayed fervently that I was not.)

I arrived feeling angry; battered and bruised by months of negative thinking, heart-rending disappointment and seemingly barren prayers. Put it this way, it was not a promising or hopeful premise for any kind of prayer time.

I unpacked with a heavy, but increasingly expectant heart.

God was already there in the room and He had left a message for me. It was in the form of a teeny tiny booklet on the table by someone called the Rev David Howell. (Who I could personally kiss for his wonderful words. If you know him please feel free to do this on my behalf. Make it a big smacker too.)

The booklet was entitled 'The Armour of God.'

I read it, thinking I knew what it would say... but God totally ambushed me. At the end of the pamphlet I stumbled across the following words:

'In the name of Jesus Christ I disclaim, renounce and totally reject all the depression, heaviness and gloom which now burdens me. I am a child of light, not of darkness. I will walk in the light as He is in the light, while the blood of Jesus cleanses me from all Sin.

May I live today in the communion of saints. I take as my companions the angels, archangels and all the company of heaven. May they surround me on every side to be my keepers and guardians.

And I claim the promised indwelling of the Holy Spirit, the Father's gift to all who ask Him. May I be his temple today that I may live to the praise of God the Father and after the pattern of Jesus Christ my Lord.

Amen.

'May the strength of God empower me
The wisdom of God direct me
The spirit of God inspire me
The love of God enfold me
The grace of God comfort me
The joy of God fill me[8]

Er... Hello!

I didn't want to feel oppressed and downhearted any more. I wanted to recover and regroup.

I said this prayer as a declaration – out loud in a shouty I'll-show-the-devil kind of voice. As if I was being filmed by secret 'sincerity cameras.'

Nothing happened at all. Not a sausage. Sigh. So I put the kettle on and looked out of the window. I may have even whistled nonchalantly.

I didn't notice the leak of the poison at first... but only half an hour later I was laughing and crying with the kind of freedom that I know only comes from a place of peace and contentment and resignation. (I know that sounds a bit tri-polar, but trust me, it was just what I needed.) I didn't want to be dogged by fears of depression and illness any longer. And I told them so. They had no choice but to leave. They were squatting in the house of my heart without my permission. So I evicted them.

I had had a sore throat for weeks (you know the kind where you have to psych yourself up to swallow?) and I slowly began to be aware that it was a spiritual and not a physical thing at all. I asked the Lord about it.

He told me that I had been swallowing lies whole. Youch! This had literally made my throat red, angry and swollen.

Right-o.

I asked Him to take my painful throat away. It eased over the next few hours and I woke up the following morning with total healing.

The three chairs opposite the sofa I sat in seemed to be occupied by presences of God that I knew were three angels. I felt truly comforted and at home with myself again.

The truth of Isaiah 26:3 'You keep him in perfect peace whose mind is stayed on you, because he trusts in you' (ERV) came flooding into my soul.

A giggle came into my spirit and I laughed out loud for the first time in months.

'Ah! Happiness!' I said, joyfully, 'I remember you! Welcome back!'

PERSPECTIVES

'So far, so good. They really seem to be bending over backwards to speed things up – which is in itself, of course, cause for alarm. But Barney said to Ems today that if they felt it was hopeless, they wouldn't be trying so hard. We'll see. Either way is good for me. Heaven soon, or heaven later.'

An email from my Mum to family and friends

I don't know what has happened to you, what you've been through. It may simply sound trite for me to say that 'God does'. But it is also incredibly and dramatically true.

He has walked every step of your life next to you and there is nothing about you that He does not know. He knows every tear you have cried and every one you have swallowed whole. He knows the times you have silently screamed into your pillow or written desperate thoughts into your journal. He was there. And He still is.

Perhaps today you feel overwhelmed by distress and sorrow. Maybe you picked up this book because you are struggling with the awful pain of fresh grief; the smell of death is raw, real, too near by half, and you hate it. Or maybe you are reading this for someone else, wondering how to break into their darkness and give them some comfort.

I don't know the reason you're here, but I am glad you are.
Thank you for coming with me.

Let me start this section of the book by saying that none of us WANTS to grieve. We don't want to be in the position where we have to. But the consequences of not grieving – when we NEED to – can be severe and damaging.

I cannot begin to guess at the reason for your anguish and I won't do you the disservice of trying. But perhaps you will find yourself somewhere on the following list.

You may be grieving because:

1. A loved one, or a number of people, have died
2. Your partner has left you
3. You are dealing with the trauma of an abortion
4. You have lost a deep friendship
5. You have lost your home
6. You have lost your health
7. You have lost your job
8. You have lost your reputation
9. You have lost a treasured relationship
10. You have lost your memory
11. You have lost your mental health
12. You are grieving someone else's pain, such as the illness of a child or partner
13. You are coping with the aftermath of a divorce
14. You have been abused in some way

I am so sorry for what you are going through and I genuinely hope that you are finding a way to come to terms with it. I am praying for you right now that this book is like a little love letter from heaven. I pray that it speaks your language and reaches the darkest recesses of your soul. (And, at the very least, that it doesn't make you want to throw it in a corner, reach for the remote control and catch up on *Home and Away*.)

I obviously can't write in detail about every scenario possible, but I hope to pick up on themes of grief that you might be feeling in your specific situation.

GRIEF IS YOUR FRIEND

It may feel like a horrible time in your life right now. You may see your grief as your enemy, as something you are doing battle with. But stop for a moment and consider this: how does Jesus ask us to treat our enemies? Do you remember? Matthew 5:44 sees him telling us to love our enemies. LOVE them. That is radical, isn't it?

Grief is not your enemy. I can promise you that. It is an honest friend. It is helping you out of one place into another better one. So learn to make friends with your grief. Allow it. Let it come. Its presence in your life should be given validity. It is not trying to make things harder.

I also want you to learn to see how you are feeling right now as a positive. Not that the way you are feeling is positive. Of course it may not be. It could be horrendous. But I want you to see that there can be good things that will come from this season.

Just cast your mind back and think for a moment about another time in your life that you found difficult. Perhaps it was a failure of some kind, a crisis or a loss.

Now ask yourself these questions:

- Did anything good come out of that situation? If so, what?
- Did that situation draw you closer to God? Or has the way you have handled it since done so?
- Have you seen a positive change in the way you pray because of it?
- Have you grown in any way because of it?
- Have you been able to help others because of what you have gone through?
- Do you have more compassion for people in similar circumstances?

I hope you can see what I am driving at.

We rarely grow spiritual or mental muscle in the sunny, easy times.

> "The most beautiful people we have known are those who have known defeat, known suffering, known struggle, known loss, and have found their way out of the depths. These people have an appreciation, a sensitivity, and an understanding of life that fills them with compassion, gentleness, and a deep loving concern. Beautiful people do not just happen."[1]

You may feel as though your life is rubbish and that you don't have anything left to live for, but that is not actually true. Is it not how things ARE. It is how things FEEL —and those are two very different things.

There is hope and I pray for you as you read this that it rises up within you.

God uses everything in our lives to make us more like Jesus. And that's all right with us most of the time, isn't it? But actually Isaiah 53:3 says that Jesus was a 'man of sorrows and acquainted with grief.' This means we are in very good company when we grieve. Jesus knew deep sorrow too and he wept. If we wish to grow in character and maturity we cannot expect to bypass all hardship, sorrow and grief. Being like Jesus sometimes means experiencing what he experienced. It means being acquainted with grief. Knowing it, like a person. A friend even.

ALL DIFFERENT

God designed grief for you and for me. In fact, it is actually a gift for us, a present to enable us to move forward. It is totally necessary for our well being after bereavement, but there is no right way to grieve, no one correct path to take.

There are certainly things that will make it easier or harder for us. And there are established patterns of grief that we might recognise in ourselves or others. (I will talk a bit more about this later in the book.) But the way we process and handle loss can look incredibly different from one person to another. Bereavement is immensely personal. We all grieve in different ways, at a different pace and with different intensity.

Even within close-knit families, each person will express emotion in their own, often contrasting, ways. One may find it helpful and cathartic to go through old photographs; another may find just the thought of that way too upsetting.

If you are grieving right now alongside others in your family, the chances are that you will not be handling it exactly like them. That can be hard to come to terms with, but is certainly worth remembering.

I was chatting to my eldest son just now and asking him if he misses his Grandma. I braced myself for any tears and hugs that would follow.

'Not really,' he said, happily. 'I have had a great week and you bought me

FIFA 13 with my pocket money, so it's all good. I'm playing football in the garden with Ben now. See you later!'

He planted a kiss on my forehead and ran off.

I swallowed hard. Sometimes we expect someone to feel something exactly the way we do, and they just plain don't. We imagine what we might feel in their place. But they don't. We project our feelings on to them and worry about them. But in fact they are not struggling with those emotions at all. Why? Because they are not us!

Occasionally, people in a family will all hit on the same note of grief together, at once. That 'note' carries such resonance for each person that it makes you sob out loud in a great noisy unison – like at a funeral when a tribute is given, for example. But those times are rare. The truth is that no one will grieve like you.

'God only knows!' is a throwaway line people use a lot in films when they don't know what to do or say. But it is true. And I am so grateful for it. We don't have to feel isolated or lonely in the way that we are grieving because we are totally understood by the Lord of all heaven.

He knows what we are going through and what we need.

Not only that – he can actually deliver the remedies we are searching for, too.

SWALLOW OR WALLOW?

When we are hurting and grieving, there are two traps we can fall into if we are not careful. At one end of the scale is the desire to block our emotions, to swallow them, hoping they will just subside on their own. Deep emotion can be scary. Most of us would prefer not to go near it and instead run a mile in the opposite direction. Some people can be especially uncomfortable when the tears are about to flow.

At university, I was in love with an amazing guy. He was adorable. I had hoped he was The One. But then one day, out of the blue, he ended our relationship. I went back to the house I shared with others, in bits. My male housemate was the only person in. (Deep joy) I sobbed my way into his bedroom and sat down on the bed. There were no tissues in the house and so I went dejectedly into the bathroom to get myself some loo roll. After briefly listening to the first part of my story, he interrupted, saying, 'Ems, please don't cry any more. That's our last bog roll and I need to go now!!'

(Incidentally, he remembers being incredibly pastoral and kind at this moment and argues vociferously that this never happened!)

Sometimes we NEED to cry, whatever others may think.

I can remember well the night my Mum was diagnosed with inoperable cancer. My friend Jen came over and we started to pray. As she and my husband laid hands on me, this powerful wail came from my belly and utterly terrified me. It lasted for ages, too. I sounded like a wounded animal, a sound I have never made before and never want to make again. But it was what I needed to let out. It was so healing and therapeutic for me (even if the neighbours may have wanted to call the RSPCA afterwards.)

Trying to 'soldier on for Jesus' is a big trap for Christians. We all want to be cope-rs and overcomers. So we try hard to be. People in church ask how we are and we say 'Yeah, getting there!' with as strong a smile as we can muster when what we really mean is that we haven't opened our eyes in the last six months without feeling a physical weight of sorrow suffocating our hearts and we have mentally tattooed the Samaritans phone number on the back of our hand.

It is unhealthy and actually unkind to ourselves to obstruct our emotions in this way. Not only that, but it shuts us out a massive channel of God's comfort – his people. In the hope of somehow protecting ourselves we can end up barricading ourselves into a bunker of self-pity and despair. People can't reach in and we can't reach out. And, as those darn good American preachers with questionable grammar say, 'That ain't no good for no one!'

God wants us to feel our emotions deeply because that is part of what it means to be human and to live life in all its fullness. Living life to the full does not mean never being sad. It means experiencing the depth and breath of any given human emotion - at the appropriate time – including sorrow.

Sorry about that. But it is the truth.

The second extreme is becoming so consumed by our sorrow that we see (and want to see) nothing else. We wallow in it. We have all been with totally depressed grief-stricken people I am sure. We can handle it for a bit ... but the umpteenth time they manage to turn an innocent conversation about a loaf of bread into a depressing story about themselves... well, we can kind of lose the will. You know?

'Mood hoovers' like this are dangerous company to keep for long. You know the kind of people who walk into a room dragging their invisible friend Abject Misery with them? So what do we do with such people? We start to avoid them. We conveniently forget to invite them out to that lovely little dinner party we are holding and we move them a tad further down our list of favourites on our phones. This isolates Little Miss Depressed even more and makes her feel as though she has no real friends, which then sends her into a self-destructive spiral of eating more Häagen-Dazs and trawling through all her rom-com DVD's, howling like a fire alarm at the sad moments.

I don't want to do this to others and I am sure you don't either. But it will happen if we wallow around in the murky water of sadness for too long.

It is really important that even when we are in the depths of grieving we take an interest in what other people are doing and needing. We may need to force ourselves to be a teensy bit sociable but we must do it. I am not suggesting we party every night, but that it would be good to meet up with close friends regularly.

NEW NORMALS

After someone close to us has died, things are not 'normal.' 'Who we are' changes and 'who other people were' when that person was around, can be different too. When my Mum died, my Dad appeared to change dramatically. The Dad I had known was one who had leant on my Mum and given her life huge meaning. Without her, he seemed like an unfamiliar person for some time. I was grieving not just my mother but who she helped others around me to be.

Our loved ones interpret family and life for us in ways we don't know about until they are gone.

My Mum was a planner and an organiser. She would think ahead and arrange to get family members together. I am a bit like that – but nowhere near as good as she was at it. I suddenly realised that if I didn't do it, it might not happen.

We want normality, but for a while after bereavement, none exists – at least, not deep down. We have to start to invent 'new normals', new traditions and helpful things that keep us balanced.

There will be people in our lives who will be better for us than others. In this season you may need to surround yourself with people who are not about to fall apart with a loud bang.

I have a good friend I see sometimes. I love her attitude to life. She describes herself as someone who 'doesn't sweat the small stuff' (and to my knowledge she doesn't sweat the big stuff much either). She is a great person to be around whatever mood I am in because she is a 'game-raiser' and a 'faith-filler.' Find people like that in your church or your family and seek them out. They are gold dust!

The best thing to do is to try and get back into some kind of normality in life again. I admire people I know who've been bereaved and who, by God's grace, continue to live unselfish and fruitful lives. They are involved with people, helping and serving others – not sitting at home watching daytime telly working their way through a family pack of Kit Kats.

Being sad with the right people is better than being happy with the wrong ones. Trust me, I have learnt that. It can cheer you up massively to be with the right people – whatever your mood. So pray that God releases people into your life who can be that for you and that you can perform that function for others, too.

During the process of writing this book, I have been very blessed to be able to stand alongside another set of close friends as they have gone through a difficult time of bereavement. It has helped me no end to think of ways to bless them during this past few weeks. I have been able to put myself in their shoes many times and try to anticipate their needs. I can't tell you how healing that has been for me.

We are called to 'comfort all who mourn'[2] and what a joy it is to know what those who mourn really need!

I have shared some of the ways you can care for others who are mourning in chapter 10.

IT'S ALL GOD'S FAULT

No matter how deep your pain or where its roots lie, God can bring you deeper comfort and hope. You may read that and think, 'He won't do that for me! He can't do that for me! I don't even WANT Him to. I am in too much of a mess! And anyway, he should have STOPPED IT!'

You may feel that and your emotions may be powerfully agreeing with you, but I want to challenge you: what if you are wrong? What if that is a misconception, and yet it is one that you are building your life on right now? Imagine for a second that God can impact your life again and shower you with his grace. Imagine that you believed that again. Imagine that you asked him back into your life to do just that. Imagine it.

However messy my life has been (and trust me, I have been in some horrible situations) God has always been there for me. The Bible speaks of Him being 'closer than a brother'.[3] I don't know whether you have brothers. I have three and I love each of them so deeply that I can't stop telling people how amazing they are. And it's mutual. We are so FOR each

'Grief
is
your
friend'

(Ems)

other. But however much they love me and support me and want the best for me, God's relationship with me trumps them all. He is closer to me than they are. He loves me more and he invests in my success more.

And so it is with confidence that I make a declaration over you right now: *You are not in too much of a mess for him to sort.* He loves you; more than your sister, or your dad or your best friend. He is here for you right now, in this moment. And he isn't going anywhere. With his help, you will find hope and healing and change. You may even struggle to deal with the fact that you will one day feel better than you do now. You may feel guilty that you are not in such a mess anymore, as if it somehow betrays the memory of the person you have lost.

THE GIFT OF SIGHT

The day we were told we were having twins, my husband and I were both in shock. My poor Jon was white as a sheet. For over an hour, all he could find to say was, 'We need a bigger car! We need a bigger car!'

But on the way back home, he saw something that really helped to shift his perspective. As we were driving through a one-way system near the hospital, he spotted some graffiti scrawled across a wall. It said:

'What you see depends on where you stand.'

It's an obvious statement but it's really profound, isn't it? It had a huge impact on him and was a word from God to us that day.

Imagine being at a gig of your choice on the front row. You see everything, a clear view of the artist you have come to watch. During one song, you see a tear roll down his or her face. It is not caught on camera so the big screens don't pick up on it. But you do. You catch that emotion. You realise that song is about some real emotion. You see it.

Your friend may be at the same gig, one or two places away from you, standing behind a security professional the size of a cruise ship, and not see it. Did it really happen? Of course it did. But one of you was not in a position to see it.

Grief is not a good position from which to see things clearly.

It makes things misty for a bit. It can cause you to miss things and misrepresent things in your mind. It can cloud your dreams and block out the light.

What you see depends on where you stand.

Robert Louis Stevenson, the author of *Treasure Island*, lived in 19th century Scotland.

> 'One night, when he was a small boy, his nanny called him to come to bed. Oblivious to her summons he was staring at something outside his nursery window. The nanny walked over, stood at his shoulder and inquired patiently, "Robert, what are you looking at?" The little boy, without taking his eyes away from the window, exclaimed in wonder as he pointed to the lamplighter who was lighting the street lamps. As Robert stood watching with fascination, his parents asked him, 'Robert, what in the world are you looking at out there?' With great excitement he exclaimed: 'Look Nanny! That man is putting holes in the darkness!'[7]

And this is what God wants to do for you right now.

Our perspective is very powerful. In a recent talk at our church, the speaker shared some research he had come across about the way we understand the world. In 2003, a psychologist called Aaron Kay conducted an experiment where he took two groups of people and exposed one set to pictures of neutral things like turkeys, kites and whales. He showed the other group fountain pens, briefcases and other items connected to the world of business. He then gave people from both groups the opportunity to negotiate a deal with another person. People in the group that had seen those 'business things' bargained harder and more aggressively. Their perspective had been shifted by their environment. What they had seen and been exposed to, changed their perception of themselves. It also changed their behaviour.

How you see things depends on your perspective.

When you look back at your life, you tend to divide your experiences and achievements in categories: positive or negative, success or failure, painful or joyful. We all make those judgements based on values the world has trained and conditioned us to hold.

You might look at your life and see nothing but pain and hopelessness right now. But just because that is the way it is now, does not mean that is how it will always stay. God wants to punch some holes in your darkness. Look at your life from the rear view mirror and things did not always turn out the way you thought, did they?

So what about your future? Could you be wrong to feel so hopeless about it? Could you be ruling yourself out of something God has ruled you in for? Could God give you the desires of your heart after all?

Forgive me for being so honest with you. I probably don't know you and may never meet you. But I think the answer is 'yes'.

If you think of every single myth or fairy tale in the world, the story always reaches a point of sheer and total hopelessness before the rescue can begin. The wolf eats Granny; the princess pricks her finger and falls asleep for 100 years; Cinderella doesn't get to go to the ball… Things look totally bleak. But then there comes a rescuer, a figure who saves the day.

God is riding on a white horse to come to your aid right now. He is about to turn your darkness into light.

What you see depends on where you stand. So where are you? How are you really? Have you taken much time to ask?

Remember that grief is God's way of working all things together for good for you right now.

What you see depends on where you stand.

And you may not even be standing right now.

ENLARGED
BY: EMS HANCOCK

BLOG
POST
JANUARY
11th
2012

I sometimes love the old language of the King James Version of the Bible. The other day I read Psalm 4 in that translation. It immediately offered a completely different take on the passage.

> 'Hear me when I call, O God of my righteousness: thou hast enlarged me when I was in distress; have mercy upon me, and hear my prayer.'[4]

Look at the same verse in the NIV:

> 'Answer me when I call to you, my righteous God. Give me relief from my distress; have mercy on me and hear my prayer.'

Not quite so amazing a translation, is it?

'Thou hast enlarged me...' sounds pretty cool to me (as long as we are talking spiritual worth and not physical girth. I don't need the other kind at all.)

My view is that God chooses to 'enlarge' us when we are in distress.

When my Mum had eye cancer, God enlarged her faith. Her witness became easy as she simply shared her story. Maybe something similar has happened for you, too.

This week I had some wonderfully healing prayer ministry. As I sat and bared my soul I realised afresh that some of the difficulties I have gone through in my past have made me stronger, braver and closer to Father God. I am *enlarged* as a result.

When God wants to grow our spiritual muscles what does He do? Firstly, He puts our muscles to the test. He gives us something heavier to carry, or wider to hold. Then he watches how we handle it. Will we moan and groan under the weight, or will we adjust well to this new way of doing life? What will happen to our faith when things don't go the way we planned? Will we collapse, blame others or will we work hard to see how God is enlarging us?

I read in my Bible notes this week that the enemy's number one target is our faith. No surprises there! Jesus said to Peter, '… Satan has asked for you, that he may sift you as wheat. But I have prayed for you, that your faith should not fail'.[5]

What a prayer!

'I have prayed for you,' says Jesus.

My notes went on to say, 'In the same way that wheat gets separated from chaff, our enemy wants to separate us from our faith. He may attack your health, but he's after your faith. He may attack your finances, but he's after your faith.'[6]

He may attack your reputation, but he is after your faith. He may attack your kids, but he is after your faith. When we realise this, what we most need to do is hide ourselves in God and pray that he will choose today to enlarge our faith.

THE FIGHT
BATTLING WITH GOD

> 'I asked God for strength, that I might achieve.
> I was made weak, that I might humbly learn to obey.
> I asked for health, that I might do greater things.
> I was given infirmity, that I might do better things.
> I asked for riches, that I might be happy.
> I was given poverty, that I might be wise.
> I asked for power, that I might have the praise of men.
> I was given weakness that I might feel the need of God.
> I asked for all things that I might enjoy life.
> I was given life, that I might enjoy all things.
> I got nothing I asked for, but everything I hoped for.
> Almost despite myself, my unspoken prayers were
> answered. I am among men richly blessed.'
>
> A confederate soldier's prayer (Author unknown)

GOD THE TRAINER

For the last few years it has felt as though I have been in some kind of wrestling match with God.

I have battled for understanding and revelation from him. I have cried out to him for comfort, grace and strength. At times I have found it hard to hear his word to me and at other times have sensed his amazing presence and promises.

Looking back, I know he never gave me half measures of anything I needed. But I also know he did not always answer my prayers the way I wanted or thought was best for me.

God's methods of comforting us can sometimes be strange and hard to fathom. He did not choose to comfort me by taking away burdens that were heavy, but instead by giving me a stronger back to carry them. He did not release me from times of trauma or trial, but walked alongside me through them. He has been training me. Just as he is training you.

When we train someone, it is always for a purpose. We potty train children in order to be able to use the toilet independently; we train athletes to perform on the track or field; we train soldiers for battle. There is always a higher purpose, a reason.

I have come to understand something very beautiful about God recently. He doesn't wrestle with us for fun, or to weaken us, or simply to bend us to his rule. He will not force us into submission. He allows us to fight with him because he wants to spend crucial time with us, revealing to us our vulnerabilities, teaching us about our destiny and helping strengthen the muscles of our faith.

I am very inspired by the U.S. Navy Seal's pledge. Part of it says:

> 'I will never quit. I persevere and thrive on adversity. My Nation expects me to be physically harder and mentally stronger than my enemies. If knocked down, I will get back up, every time. I will draw on every remaining ounce of strength to protect my teammates and to accomplish our mission. I am never out of the fight.'[1]

There is something very biblical about that covenant promise, isn't there? I think God is teaching me to keep getting back up too.

WRESTLING

The story of how Jacob wrestled with God, found in Genesis 32, fascinates me. It is actually rather difficult to understand at face value. Why would God hurt Jacob? Why would he not allow himself to 'win'? Why wrestle all night with a human being anyway? There are some tricky questions there.

As I have dwelt on this passage over the last few months, I have learnt some really important lessons about the way God has handled me and the things he has deposited in me.

Some commentators say that Jacob grappled with God himself and others think it was an angel. The prophet Hosea describes it like this:

'In the womb he grasped his brother's heel; as a man he struggled with God. He struggled with the angel and overcame him; he wept and begged for his favour.'[2]

Notice that we are *not* told that Jacob wrestled with a man. What it says is that the man (or angel) wrestled with Jacob. Is it significant that it is this way round? I think so. It shows us that *God* is the initiator of this conflict. It tells us that God started a fight! As F.B. Meyer writes, 'It was as though God knew it was his only chance. He wanted to lift Jacob up to a new royal life, and so he actually wrestled with him as though to compel him to yield to him.'[3]

Does any of that sound familiar in your life, too?

But the question remains, how could a mere human like Jacob fight a supernatural being for *any* length of time? How is it possible that the Lord, or one of his mighty angels, could not immediately overpower Jacob (v. 25)? It is an important question. Is God ever weaker than man? Is God ever nearly beaten?

Well, not the God I know. No.

GOD, THE PROVOKER

I believe he chose to allow Jacob to believe he could win.

Why?

Because there is something very intimate about a fight. There is closeness, eye contact, physicality, mud, humanity, touch, struggle, heartache and breath. Nothing can be hidden. In it we see God allowing something incredible to take place: 'FaceTime' with himself.

I want you to understand something again with me. The supernatural man (or angel of God) had the power to disable Jacob at *any* time. So why didn't he just beat him and leave him to realise that you don't mess with God?

Because our God is not like that, is he?

I believe God wanted to impart something of intimacy to Jacob – albeit in rather a bizarre way!

When it began to get light and the angel wanted to leave, all he had to do was touch Jacob's hip socket and it wrenched completely out of place. Let's all pause to say 'ouch.' I am currently having physio for a neck problem and know well the pain of any kind of joint manipulation. But dislocation? That's a whole other level of pain. The Hebrew word used here certainly can mean 'dislocated'. I checked.

Again: 'ouch'.

So why did the angel wait for a whole night before inflicting the final blow? Perhaps he was biding his time until he knew Jacob had used up and fought with all his strength and come to the end of his struggle. Whatever the reason, the fight was certainly necessary both for Jacob's transformation and his revelation.

At the point where Jacob was exhausted and had nothing more to fight with, the angel relieves him of his equilibrium and his usual gait. He changes the way he walks.

The message is pretty clear: 'You have striven with all your might. Yet, with one single touch I can defeat you.' Jacob needed to see the superiority of his opponent with eye-watering, painful clarity. And how often have we experienced the same?

How often does God need to remind us that we don't control our own destiny and that without him we are, and have, nothing? (In my case, quite often!)

Jacob knew the right words and could perform the right actions. But his heart still did not belong completely to the Lord. And they both knew it. The fight proved it.

It's easy to have superficial faith. We all know people who used to come along to church who now don't. For some reason, life got the better of them. Fair-weather faith disappears the minute a storm brews or something more attractive lures us away. However, a crisis forces us to grapple with our real feelings and the extent of our faith. The storm proves the depth and strength of what we believe.

What I am about to say will hardly ever be preached about. It is a very unpopular theology in our feel-good, nice-God western church culture.

I believe that the people God loves deeply he provokes deeply.

Let me say that again, another way. If God loves you, he will bring (or allow) trouble to fall upon you. Is that a revelation to you? Is that an horrific and unpalatable proposition to you?

Well, I can assure you, it's a very biblical one. Look at Daniel. Joseph. Moses. David. Abraham. Even Jesus.

There is no doubt that God loved these people. Enormously. And yet that love encompassed huge struggles, problems, pain and difficulty, too.

See? God causes and allows trouble for his favourites.

GOD, THE PROTECTOR

Let me describe it in another way.

I have, more than once, deliberately allowed another human being to cause pain to one of my children. Before you ring ChildLine, listen to the context. I allowed a nurse to give my children vaccinations.

Did it hurt? *Yes.*
Did they like it? *No.*
Did they understand it? *No.*
Did they need it? *Yes.*

I believe God sometimes uses pain to vaccinate us, to help us cling on to him more fully and protect us from what is coming next.

He may well be looking for a fight with you right now because he wants to get you ready for something only He can see coming. God provokes this fight with Jacob to bring him to a point of genuine faith. That is why he provokes crises for you and me, too. He may well be using what is happening in your life right now to cause you to react.

And when he does this, it is not pleasant, easily comprehensible or enjoyable. But it is totally *necessary* – for our long-term faith, our well being and our character.

When Jacob called out for a blessing from God, the wall had been broken down. Blessing could finally flow again. He knew who he was dealing with and what he needed God to do. Blessing means release.

It means the end of the fight, but the start of living, the beginning of the new adventure.

God did not just want Jacob's outward worship; he wanted his inward devotion. And he wants the same from us.

He is really not all that interested in what we say in church, or to the babysitter about how wonderful our kids are. Or what we pretend to be in front of the boss. He wants honest reality. The real us. Even the 'us' that wants to fight back.

Back to our amazing story. Why do you think that the angel asks Jacob for his name (v.27)?

Do you find this question ever so slightly odd? I do. I mean, he knew it already, didn't he? If this is God's messenger (and I totally believe it is) shouldn't he already know Jacob's name without having to ask it?

Listen to the words of Ravi Zacharias as he explains it:

> 'Think of all that God could have said by way of reprimand. Instead he merely asks for Jacob's name. God's purpose in raising this question contains a lesson for all of us, too profound to ignore. In fact, it dramatically altered Old Testament history. In asking for the blessing from God, Jacob was compelled by God's question to relive the last time he had asked for a blessing, the one he had STOLEN from his brother.
>
> 'The last time Jacob was asked for his name, the question had come from his earthly father. Jacob had lied on that occasion and said, "I am Esau," and stole the blessing. Now he found himself, after

many wasted years of running through life looking over his shoulder, before an all-knowing, all-seeing heavenly Father, once more seeking a blessing, Jacob fully understood the reason and the indictment behind God's question and he answered, "My name is Jacob."

"You have spoken the truth," God said, "and you know very well what your name signifies. You have been a duplicitous man, deceiving everyone everywhere you went. But now that you acknowledge the real you, I can change you, and I will make a great nation out of you."'

Amazing, isn't it?

So why did God choose to hurt Jacob's hip in this bizarre encounter? I think the answer to this question may well be this: scars remind us of what we have been through and what we have learned. Just like a wedding ring reminds us who we are married to, who we must cherish and love each day, so our scars remind us of our need for God, what he has brought us through.

Perhaps you have had, or are still having a wrestling match with God in your life. Perhaps you now feel you walk with a pronounced limp.

I am learning that my greatest problem is not the circumstances of my life but my attitude towards those circumstances.

I am also learning that in any struggle, and particularly in my time of grief, that God is my strength and my hope, that he can carry my full weight – the depth of my questions, anger, failure, fears, frailty and doubts. What is more, the presence of all those things in me does not impact or alter the fact that he loves me *one tiny bit.*

So don't be alarmed. Don't fear such encounters with the Lord. If you are battling with him right now, questioning him, shouting at him, struggling with him, he understands.

This situation may feel like it is breaking you, but with God's grace it will also be the making of you.

THIS WILL BE THE DEATH OF ME

How do you feel about your personal future? For months after my Mum died, I felt as though I had died, too.

In fact on a number of occasions, my Gran, who suffered with dementia in her last few years on earth, bemoaned, 'Isn't it awful that Emma has died?' getting me confused with Mum.

But I would not disagree with her. I would hold and pat her hand, with tears rolling down my face and say, 'Yes. It is awful darling.'

I felt as though my best years were behind me, that my dreams were as good as dead and that I had been wrong and foolish to dream them in the first place. I felt that for the rest of my days I would be nothing more than a carer – either for my Gran, or my Dad, or my brothers, or my husband or my kids. I am not saying that the role of carer is not a calling, or a valuable life's work. But it was not my personal dream.

One of the ugly stepsisters of grief is this kind of inner confusion. I don't know why grief did this to me, but I understand it is a common thread for many people after bereavement. Life just doesn't seem to make sense. Our dreams are rocked and our worlds are shattered. Lots of things we have taken for granted need re-thinking. Many of us find that our energies are depleted and anything over and above day-to-day survival seems impossible. I looked up some of the prophecies that had been spoken over my life and what I thought I would be doing by the age of 40 and there was absolutely no correlation with reality. I felt cheated and let down. Had I missed my path? Had the ship sailed without me? It certainly felt like it.

I am not really the kind of person who suffers from 'comparison-itis'. I am one of the most secure people I know. I do not suffer from anxiety about my gifts or lack of them. I know myself pretty well. I am a confident woman, on the whole. But in this season of my life I began to look around me with envy. Other people seemed to be achieving great things for God with comparative ease. My abortive attempts at serving him seemed to have amounted to very little.

I gave up thinking God had anything else for me. Other people's needs overtook my own and left nothing of me behind. I was fully spent every day in looking after others and making sure each had what they needed.

As we organised my Mum's funeral, I battled my personal inabilities to work through the finances and legal papers (which, incidentally, a year later, is still an almost weekly task). I dealt with jewellery, clothes and personal belongings.

I had only just finished sorting all of Mum's things out, when Gran died and I felt like I had to start all over again. My life felt like it was well and truly over.

I stopped meeting up with people to mentor them –something I have intentionally done with huge joy for years and years. Who was I to give advice and pray for others when I was in such inner turmoil and had no energy or time to stand alongside anyone outside the family? This is what I felt.

I also felt God was asking me to put down my singing. For a while, and for no reason I could fathom, there seemed to be a total lack of favour over anything I attempted musically. Musicians I contacted to play with me for various things would either not respond at all or display indifference to my music. It was very hard and not a little humbling. It felt like a consistently shut door that I was trying to prize open with a thin plastic knife.

So I prayed and felt it was right to simply stop. I stepped down from my occasional attempts at leading worship and stopped any other singing, too. As I made this seismic personal sacrifice in obedience to God, many people seemed not to notice. Again, this was very humbling.

The moment I stopped trying to make things happen for myself in this area I felt a huge sense of relief. I had been asking God to do something in my life that he plainly didn't want to do at that time. I had been sad about it for months. Suddenly it was gone!

I did not turn any music on in the house for half a year. Music had been my solace, my comfort, part of my spiritual armour and my passion for almost as long as I could remember, but somehow, and for some reason I can't fully explain, I could not handle it any more. Those who know me well understand that I spent hours listening to music as I prayed. But during this time, I just couldn't bring myself to switch it on. Those were quiet, sad months.

I changed the label in my head and in my heart. At a party someone said, 'Are you Ems Hancock, the singer?'

'I am Ems Hancock, but I am not a singer,' I said.

Perhaps it was because Mum always called me her 'Songbird'? Perhaps it was because she was my greatest encourager musically and she was gone. I honestly don't know.

It all seemed hopeless for me.

If I was not a singer, who was I?

DESIGNER LABEL

A funny thing happened the day God healed me of my sore throat and dealt with the spirit of gloom I spoke about in Chapter 1. He asked me a question: 'Do you think I like your music?'

I confess I had never thought about it before. I have written songs for years now – simple songs, some better than others, but yes, songs.

Truthfully, I didn't really want to think about the answer. It was too significant. Too painful.

'I don't know,' I fluffed.

God asked me to turn on my phone and replay some old songs that I had not been able to listen to without huge pain. I didn't want to, and I begged him to let me listen to something else, someone else instead, but he wanted me to hear my own voice. It was uncomfortable, to say the least.

A line from one of my own spontaneous songs came over very powerfully to me:

'*My best is yet to come.*'

Did I truly believe that?

Not really. Not any more.

I could believe it for everyone else around me: my friends, my husband, my brothers and my kids. Even my Dad. Just not me.

I was hurt that I had wasted years of my life believing I would be a Christian singer. Suddenly I felt that I was faced with the possibility that God may have never intended me to think of myself in these terms at all, that the albums I had recorded were a giant lesson in humility, not success. Perhaps my dreams had been drip-fed to me by well-meaning Christians seeking to encourage me, rather than by God? To be honest, even as I write this, I am not sure.

I understand that nothing is wasted and that God wonderfully and carefully uses every circumstance of our lives to teach us and equip us for whatever he plans next. I'm really not sure if my future contains anything musical and I guess only time will tell. I certainly don't want to rule anything out forever just because it is hard to deal with, and harder to explain, now. But I am not waiting around for something to begin that may never happen. I also feel I have begun to learn that my imagination is capable of being both beautiful and also deeply flawed. I have run ahead of God on many occasions and joined the dots of the picture, without waiting for him. I have made assumptions about the direction my life is going in based on the evidence of what I can see and understand. But God's ways are not restricted to these pathways.

It is normal for grief to change the landscape of our lives like this. Understandably, God wants us to put certain things down in order to heal us. He needs us to have empty hands before he will fill them again. Whilst it can be painful to be obedient to him – especially when we don't understand why he is asking us to do something – simple obedience will always bring blessing and ultimately deep contentment.

I no longer miss singing the way I did a year ago. I am not unkind or negative about myself in this area any more. I am even occasionally able to listen to an old song without anger, sadness or regret. I think this is progress.

As I was writing this chapter, the current Bishop of Liverpool, James Jones, was being interviewed on BBC Radio 2. He described how, whilst on a skiing holiday years ago God had called him to be ordained as a priest. Everything in him wanted to rebel: he was just about to get married and had planned a career in something else. As he got on a ski lift he noticed that he was totally alone. There was no one else on the mountain. So he shouted at God, at the top of his voice:

'OK, then! I will do what you ask!'

He wasn't shouting with delight or obedience, but in the way a grumpy, wilful child feels when he is made to say sorry to another child before he is ready. He shouted angrily, wearily and with resignation. But he described what happened next as a total transformation. In that moment he was suddenly touched with love and peace, as the power of God came upon him powerfully. It was as though the battle for control was finally over. He knew God had chosen the best path for him. He gratefully submitted and came down the mountain with an open, changed heart.

I know something of this kind of declaration and this journey, too.

To be 'in submission' to God means to come under ('sub') his mission for our lives – to see that mission as our delight and shelter, not as the spoiler of our fun or our true destiny. The Bible is so clear that God has good plans for us – plans to prosper us, not to harm us. Plans for our future and works designed in advance for us to do.[4]

If we truly understood that, especially in our times of disappointment and grief we would be better at allowing his plans for us – rather than aggravating or arguing with them.

I know God is carrying me, and I hope I am becoming easier for him to lift.

DECLARATIONS AND LIES

I have learnt the hard way in this season that what we speak over ourselves and our lives really matters.

Job 22:28 says 'You will also declare a thing, and it will be established for you.'[5] If we declare something to be hopeless, we will fulfil that prophecy. But if we speak with faith, hope and trust, that will impact us, and the situation.

My recent UCB notes, "Word for Today" said, 'It's not what others say to you or about you that determine your future. It's what you say to yourself when others have finished speaking.'[6]

What kinds of things do you say over yourself when no one else is listening? Are they words of blessing, or words of blame? Things that would build you up, or tear you down?

As I started to look hard at some of my journal entries, my eyes welled up with disbelieving tears. I was writing such awful things about myself. I was declaring lies as though they were truth. In this way, I was habitually and regularly disagreeing with God and his words of life to me.

The Bible says, 'Death and life are in the power of the tongue, and those who love it will eat its fruit.'[7] Until we learn to replace our negative self-talk with words of life, we will not move forward.

WHAT SEEDS ARE YOU SOWING?

In his song, 'I Was Brought To My Senses', Sting includes the line:

'Inside every turning leaf is the pattern of an older tree.'[8]

I have never got over the miracle contained in a seed. It is crazy to think that massive oak trees come from miniscule acorns.

Whatever seeds we sow and nurture in our hearts will grow. Our mind is powerful. But it is not as powerful as our hearts. If we believe something

NURTURE HAPPY SEEDS

EMS HANCOCK

in our hearts, we will become it. Proverbs says: 'As a man thinks in his heart, so he is.'[9]

As a keen gardener will decide which plants he wants to thrive in his garden, and which he does not, there must be intentionality about the business of sowing. If you don't want what a seed will ultimately produce, you must stop sowing it, feeding it, giving it room or the right conditions to thrive.

If you want to believe you will get married, but all you ever say over yourself is, 'I will never find anyone' or 'No one will choose me', you are not leaving room in your spirit for seeds of thought like 'God is preparing someone for me right now.' You are nurturing other seeds, blocking out the light for ones God may be trying to grow.

There are things I won't allow myself to say out loud or even in the stillness of my mind about myself. I won't allow myself to say, 'God will never use my singing' or 'I will never be the speaker I have dreamed of becoming', because one day he just might. I don't know! And, to be honest, it doesn't matter to me nearly as much as it used to.

I don't think God ever wanted singing or speaking or anything else to become my label. I think he always called me his child, not his singer.

He doesn't love me for what I can do but for who I am. My identity is not wrapped up in my ability or success or indeed in my lack of those things, but in who he is. A Chanel dress will have a label just like a Primark one, but one is a designer dress. We each have a designer label attached to us. This is what gives us our indescribable worth.

Many of us struggle with this, simply because it comes from the opposite thinking from that which we receive in the world. One of the very first questions people tend to ask us is, 'What do you do?'

I have tried out a few different answers recently.

I tried answering, 'Nothing.' But that didn't go down well and was also not strictly true.

I have tried, 'I am a full time Mum, part-time author and part-time cake baker.'

Better, but it still leaves out so many things.

What about, 'I am a child of the King.'

Accurate, but definitely likely to induce vomit.

Anything that just says what we do, or our job title is not really who we are. It leaves out the detail. I don't want to be defined and confined any more.

The problem with a talent programme like *The Voice* is that it is looking for a commodity. Its very title doesn't take into account what is wrapped around a voice – the person, the set of gifts, the experiences, the flaws. We are all far more than the sum of our parts.

EMPTY BOXES

For the last few months I have, almost as an act of worship, had a calendar on display in my kitchen that has remained totally blank. The white boxes that would have once been filled with activity, people and busyness have been empty.

I am trying to teach myself that my status and validity isn't based on how useful I am to others, how full my diary is or how many times a day someone 'hearts' my latest photo on Instagram.

It takes self-awareness, discipline and a good deal of reprogramming to bring our thought lives back in line with God's Word. I am learning that my inner self accepts what it is consistently fed and begins to act accordingly. I am reprogramming my heart to believe in myself in a different way.

I am trying to think what God may be planting and vigorously make room for it.

BEREAVEMENT
PATTERNS OF GRIEF

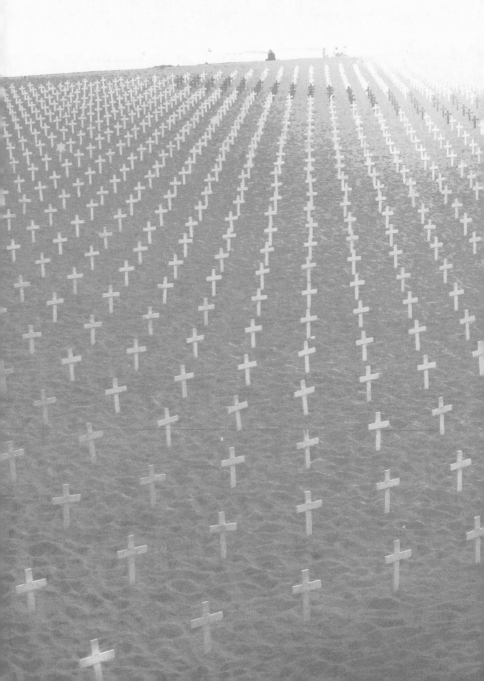

> 'Be gracious to me, O Lord, for I am in distress; my eye
> is wasted from grief; my soul and my body also. For my
> life is spent with sorrow, and my years with sighing;
> my strength fails because of my iniquity, and my bones
> waste away.'
>
> Psalm 31:9–10[1]

Understanding the nature of grief can help us cope better with our hurts. We know that grief is a feeling of deep mental anguish caused by loss. It may not come about because of a death; there are many other kinds of disappointment that can leave us needing to grieve. Grief can be triggered by the loss of possessions, of health, of a career, or sorrow for something that someone has done or failed to do.

Grief is a natural, healthy process designed by God to enable us to recover from difficult emotional wounds. William Cowper, the English hymn writer, said, 'Grief is itself medicine.' We should not feel guilty for grieving because it is a necessary and God-given part of our journey towards wellbeing and true inner healing.

A STORMY SEA

The grief process has been likened to many things. As someone who thinks in pictures, I find it useful to think of it as sailing across a sea. When we first experience the death of someone we love, or the loss of a dream, we are launched into an unfamiliar stretch of water. At first we do not know what we are feeling and there may be a sense of numbness and disbelief.

Soon however, this feeling may well be interrupted by a sensation of being suddenly engulfed in a tempest of deep-seated and sometimes highly conflicting emotions. We can feel surrounded by darkness and heavy waves of despair, tossed around by high waves, up and down, with no stillness. We want to get off the boat but we don't know how. Comforting words and even the things we want to believe about ourselves and God can be drowned out by the noise and wind of our sorrow.

With each day that passes we feel further from the shore and more confused about where we are going. We feel lonely and out of control as we are swept toward a new place – a place we never asked to go.

Perhaps if you are grieving you will be able to identify with this image. For me, it is one of the most simple and yet profound ones I have come across to date. It certainly sums up a great deal of truth about how I felt some months ago.

THE GRIEVING PROCESS

So what else can we expect when we are grieving?

Everyone is different, but there are some common patterns people go through in grief:

Shock – Shock is a natural 'cushion' designed by God. It kicks in, in order to help us begin to handle the effects of some kind of trauma. In the time after bereavement, people often report feeling numb, as though suspended in some kind of bad dream. The reality of events has not yet had time to register and you can even feel on a weird spiritual high through this stage.

Reality – As reality dawns, deep sorrow sets in accompanied by weeping and other forms of emotional release. Loneliness and depression may also occur. You can feel bleak about the future and hurt about the past, too.

Reaction – You may start to feel some anger, brought on by feelings of abandonment and helplessness. This may be directed toward family, friends, doctors, the one who died or deserted you, yourself, or even God. Other typical feelings include listlessness, apathy, and guilt over perceived failures or unresolved personal issues.

Recovery – Finally, there is a gradual, almost imperceptible return to some kind of new normality. This is a time of adjustment to the new circumstances in life.

These stages will vary in duration for each person and there is no right 'timetable' to follow. Some people go through these emotions in around a year or two; others will take less or much more time.

I remember meeting a lady in her late fifties after a talk I gave. She told me that she had been raped by a pastor when she was 15 and never told anyone. She had been so traumatised by the experience she had not allowed herself to 'feel anything' – she had never cried about it or allowed herself to think about it for long.

She had forgiven the man in question who had gone on to become a well known, successful missionary. Her grief came upon her that day as we prayed in a huge and terrifying flood. The relief that followed was immense. I felt so deeply sorry for her that she had carried it on her own for so long.

Experiencing holidays, anniversaries and birthdays without our loved one can trigger intense grief, especially during the first year of our grieving. But sometimes, just when we are expecting ourselves to feel sad, we may not. At other times grief will sneak up on us as we see a card 'To my beloved wife' in a shop, or witness a father and son having a special hug, or giggle together. Our eyes well with tears and all of a sudden we are choking with unwelcome emotion.

The healing of our brokenness in this way is similar to the healing of a broken bone. Trying to hurry the process along can actually hinder full recovery, like removing a cast before the bone is strong enough to bear weight. But keeping a cast on for too long is also damaging and can result in hampered growth, changes in muscle function and long term weakness.

Grief will take its sweet (and sour) time. And we must let it.

HOW THE WORLD GRIEVES

> 'Once upon a time children were taught to recite the Ten commandments. Learning them was regarded as a matter of mental and spiritual hygiene... It is very different nowadays. Some have never heard of them... This is sadder than we realise. All of the ten commandments are health rules. If we break them, either deliberately or out of ignorance, we invite sickness at many levels of our being.'
>
> Roy Lawrence[2]

In Britain especially, but in other countries too, we have a culture that invites sickness in this way. As a nation and as a world we don't handle grief, disappointment and loss well.

'Man up!'
'Get on with it!'
'Big girls don't cry!'
'Pull yourself together'

Phrases like these are all part of our 'stiff-upper-lip' way of life. We are ill-prepared as a society for death because we do not face it or talk about it openly. We are more likely to go on a First Aid course to know how to protect life, than to go on a bereavement course to consider death. And yet chances are, we are much more likely to face death than to ever need to give CPR.

John W James in his book *The Grief Recovery Handbook* describes how, 'We are even advised not to learn about dealing with loss – or at the very least, not to talk about it. "What's done is done." "You have to move on." "Don't burden others with your feelings." The list goes on.'[3]

We are taught and encouraged to acquire and amass 'things', but not what to do if and when we lose them. The multi-billion pound advertisement industry exists to whet our appetite for the next generation of smartphone, the biggest car or the most expensive and outrageously named perfume. But there is precious little information about what to do when these things are taken from us.

Aside from the offer of litigation and the endless, 'Have you had an accident that was not your fault?' adverts, we just aren't made ready to lose anything. Whether that be a relationship, job, boyfriend, reputation or even a sports match.

As a child I grew up with three brothers and a father who all had an obsession with the 'beautiful game' of football. Very often as we watched the endless matches shown during each season, we saw grown men totally unable to handle the total devastation of another man on the opposing team kicking a ball into a net. It is alarming that this kind of emotionally stunted behaviour is considered completely normal! Sulking, tears, fights and mobs of angry so-called fans, could all be a normal part of weekend afternoon viewing.

I love a good game of football but I despise the fact that many so-called sportsmen show so little sportsmanship. People in our culture are rarely taught to win humbly or lose gracefully. Those health lessons of the Ten Commandments aren't even a distant memory in our society. They are just distant.

Some degree of loss in our lives is inevitable. As we grow older we may lose some of our sight, our hearing or our health. We will start to lose older family members, or maybe even some relationships. But we aren't ready to do so. We think it is our right to hold on to everything we want to, for as long as we want. We get angry at the mere thought of it not being so. We are a throwaway culture that discards nappies, food and relationships on a whim. But only when we want to. We don't like these things being taken from us.

UNHEALTHY GRIEF

Sometimes in an attempt to understand and come to terms with bereavement, two unhealthy patterns can form. The first is to create some kind of impenetrable shrine to the person we have lost.

Take Helen (not her real name), for example. Helen is a lady I know in her late forties who never married. When her mother became ill she moved in to nurse her. Years later, her mother died. Helen was so attached to her mother that she never wanted to change anything in the house. She kept everything exactly as it was when her mother was alive, including the slippers by the bathroom door and the used, bent toothbrush in the cup. She never had the courage to go through her mum's clothes or belongings and felt as though it would be somehow disrespectful to do so.

Helen had been grieving in her own way for years but had not moved on because the thought of losing her grief would be too traumatic. It was all she had left of her mum. She tiptoed around the house trying hard not to get in the way of her mum's memory and her belongings. Her emotional clock was standing still.

The second unhealthy pattern people can form is to 'mouth off' about the person and be utterly unwilling to let go of any hurts and disappointments associated with them.

I recently watched a documentary about young people in prison. One girl sat in her cell shouting and screaming about how much she hated her mother and how much she didn't love her or care about her anymore. But I wasn't buying the act. Nor were the filmmakers. The very fact that she needed to say these things out loud so often showed there was no sense of moving on. She *did* love her mum and she was hurt she was no longer there. She just didn't have the language or emotional maturity to express that.

Both of these kinds of grief are incredibly real, but also disastrously limited. The first, because it is not a balanced and accurate portrayal of the deceased, and the second, well, for the very same reason.

Not 'speaking ill of the dead' or being determined to do only that, are both unhelpful and extreme stances to take. No one has ever been an entirely good or an entirely bad person and seeing them as nothing short of a god or a devil figure is misleading and damaging.

BURYING

There are of course many other unhelpful things people do when they are grieving to try and numb themselves against pain. Some try and find solace in overwork, alcohol, a drug, smoking, overeating, an affair or a new obsession like pornography, gambling or internet gaming.

Interestingly, one of the common verbal associations people make at a time like this is 'I buried myself' in drink or one of the above. To 'bury oneself' is a deeply unpleasant image. It means to hide, to go underground, to try to disappear – in some way, to create another death. None of these things sounds like a good way to grieve to me.

A few months after my Mum died, my Dad went into a frenzy of activity. Desperate not to be alone or be at a loose end for any length of time, he flung himself into every meeting and activity going. His diary was a solid scrawl of pencil markings flinging him from one place to another with very little time in between. He would then fall into bed at the end of the day and hope to sleep from sheer exhaustion, if not peace. But it wasn't good for him to be living life at such a constant and demanding pace. He was trying to avoid thinking and feeling and grieving... *because grieving is so flippin' hard.*

The trouble is, grief can wait. It will wait years and years if it has to. It is a very patient and long-suffering companion.

I sat down with my Dad and explained to him that whilst I could see that he found great comfort in being useful and being able to bless others and that this was a legitimate part of his own healing, he needed to do that from a place being filled and not being empty. I have been delighted to watch him begin to change the balance and start to take much better care of himself in recent months.

My own problems with food began again with a vengeance following the death of my Gran. Ever since I can remember, I have had an eating disorder. I hoped it had been sorted after Mum died because I stayed on a Daniel Fast (only fruit, vegetables, nuts and seeds) for eight months. I thought I was cured. But sadly the death of my Gran proved I was very wrong. I started overeating again to the point that I was disgusted by myself. At first it was comforting to have an extra bit of cake, but it soon became alarming that I wanted the whole bally thing. I watched the pounds leap onto my (already not wildly thin) body. Weighing myself four months after she had died I found that I had put on almost two stone.

We can all have unhealthy ways to express our sadness and we need God's help to stay balanced and focused on what is helpful for us. One of the verses God has given me time and time again in these days is, 'There is now no condemnation for those who are in Christ Jesus' (Romans 8:1). I am having to learn to agree with God on that and not heap condemnation on myself for my lack of discipline in what I allow into my body.

As I write, I am praying into my own situation and asking God to heal me and help me in my weaknesses. I have even resorted to making myself write a food diary to help me become totally aware of all I am consuming.

'The story is told of man who while walking down a country lane came across a stone quarry in which a number of men were working. He questioned several of them about what they were doing. The first replied irritably. 'Can't you see? I'm hewing stone.' The second answered without looking up, 'I'm earning a £100 a week.' But when the same question was put to the third man, he stopped and said, 'If you want to know what I am doing, I'm building a cathedral.' So it is a matter of how far we can see. The first man could not see beyond his pick and the second man could not see beyond his Friday pay-packet. But the third man looked beyond his tools and his wages to the ultimate end he was serving. He was co-operating with the architect. However small his particular contribution, he was helping to construct a building for the worship of God.'
John Stott[4]

God wants us to be a temple – a cathedral if you will – for him to dwell in. He can use anything, even our own sorrow and disappointment to construct the walls and floors of that building.

First Peter 5:10 describes for me, perhaps better than any other verse, what God hopes for us after a period of grief or loss: 'And the God of all grace who called you to his eternal glory in Christ, after you have suffered a little while, will Himself restore you and make you strong, firm and steadfast.'[5]

Just looking at these verses is comforting! God is a God of grace. He is not shouting at me from the sidelines of my life saying, 'What was that?! Why did you do that? Put down the crisps you idiot!' He reminds us again in this passage that he has called us to eternal glory, not eternal disgrace and shame.

He knows that we suffer, but he makes sure it is only for 'a little while.'

Some of you may be thinking, 'Ems, my so-called 'little while' has been going on for years now. When will it ever end?'

I am afraid there are no magic answers to that. I don't know any formulas to life. We know that good things happen to bad people and vice versa. It doesn't make sense to us because our understanding is so limited.

Just as I have been working on this chapter this morning, a text came in from one of my brothers. He was due to go to a wedding today but the bride died yesterday. I read those words in disbelief. How could this have happened? How can God allow such heartache and loss on a day when the family is meant to be happy and joyful?

I do not know, and to spout a simple Bible verse would be chillingly heartless. But I was in the middle of this verse when he texted and so through my tears I say over myself and this family: 'And the God of all grace who called you to his eternal glory in Christ, after you have suffered a little while, will Himself restore you and make you strong, firm and steadfast.'

It is my prayer for them, for the groom, the family and all their friends on their way right now to a wedding that isn't happening.

He reminds us in this promise that he himself will 'restore, make (us) strong, firm and steadfast.' He doesn't leave his angels or other Christians to do this. He sees it as his job. Aren't you glad that you and I are God's priority? I am.

Looking more deeply at these promises, he will:

Restore us, not to our original condition but to his original INTENTION. He will give us something better than what we have lost – if not now, certainly in heaven.

Make us strong, not so that nothing else will ever happen to us, but so that if and when it does, we will not be weakened or taken down by it.

Make us firm, not so that things won't affect or hurt us, but so that we are not shaken long term or put off course by them.

Make us steadfast, not so that we are arrogant, but so that we know he is the rock we stand on and that it is only by his power that we remain upright.

I don't know what habits you have found forming in these last few months. Perhaps, if you are truly honest, there are some patterns in your behaviour that show you are not grieving in a way that is totally healthy for you. If you could change one of those habits now, which one would it be and why?

Write it down and seek God about it. He wants to give you authority and power over that issue because he wants 'no weapon formed against you' to prosper.

COMFORT IN GOD
BY: EMS HANCOCK

BLOG
POST
MAY
9th
2012

My reading today was from Psalm 112:

'Praise the Lord.
Blessed are those who fear the Lord,
who find great delight in his commands.
Their children will be mighty in the land;
the generation of the upright will be
blessed.
Wealth and riches are in their houses,
and their righteousness endures forever.
Even in darkness light dawns for the
upright,
for those who are gracious and compassionate
and righteous.
Good will come to those who are generous
and lend freely,
who conduct their affairs with justice.
Surely the righteous will never be shaken;
they will be remembered forever.
They will have no fear of bad news;
their hearts are steadfast, trusting in
the Lord.
Their hearts are secure, they will have
no fear;
in the end they will look in triumph on
their foes.'[6]

So today, the day we will find out the prognosis for my Mum's cancer, I will have no fear of bad news and my heart will be steadfast, trusting the Lord. My heart will be secure. Why?

Because I know that he is FOR ME. He is FOR US as a family. Even if we fail him, or doubt him or are challenged in our beliefs about him. He is unwavering. He is good and his heart is to do us good, too.

In every season and circumstance of the soul, God is FOR US. I bear testimony of this truth today and I stand on a rock that ain't going anywhere.

How Christians grieve is very different to how those who do not believe face bereavement. This is not because we are immune to sadness or not in touch with our feelings but because our faith gives us hope about where our loved one is and who we are in relationship with, our Father God.

It does not mean that we should not cry and grieve. In fact, it sets us free to have good grief, the kind that is helpful, healing and restoring.

Normal grief can have many symptoms:
Trouble sleeping,
Increased anxiety,
Regrets about things that were not said or done,
Fear about the future,
Tears and weeping,
Anger and bitterness directed towards God, the person who has died, or others,
Lack of concentration,
Depression,
Numbness ,
Manic activity,
Loneliness and isolation,
Eating patterns changing – struggling to eat, or over-eating,
Mood swings and short temperedness,
Physical aches and pains.

None of these is out of the ordinary. Just being a Christian does not mean you won't feel these things. You probably won't feel all of them, but it is quite normal to feel most of them at one time or another.

I have found great comfort in the knowledge that God is caring for me as I grieve. He is not leaving me alone and hoping I will get through it on my own. Psalm 23, says, 'Even though I walk through the valley of the shadow of death, I will fear no evil. For you are with me, your rod and your staff they comfort me.'[7]

God can even comfort us in truly miraculous ways.

'MY LIFE IS SPENT WITH SORROW'

PSALM 31:10

ABIDE WITH ME
BY: EMS HANCOCK

BLOG
POST
MAY
31th
2012

Yesterday we went to the hospital and were told the devastating news that Mum's cancer is widespread and that she doesn't have long left.

Mum and Dad handled the consultation with real dignity and strength and there was a great peace in the room as we heard the findings of the tests. We had the chance to pray together afterwards and then walked out of the hospital humming 'Bless the Lord, oh my soul.' (In characteristic of my parents and myself, soft three part harmony.)

Later on, my best friend Jen popped round to comfort me. As soon as we went into the lounge and sat down we heard a loud rendition of the hymn, 'Abide with me' start up from somewhere outside. None of us could work out where it was coming from. We checked the TV (off) the laptop (not playing) and listened to see if it was coming from next door (unlikely).

In the end, Jon went outside, expecting that someone had put a speaker with it playing right outside our house (although why they would do that was beyond us, as no-one knew what had happened). But he went out to find nothing and no one there.

All of us kept asking each other 'Can you hear this?!' We all thought we were going a bit mad. But somehow, carried on the wind, we heard the whole hymn.

It was so comforting for me and I felt as though angels had been placed in the breeze to sing it to me. (Although perhaps it was coming from the church across the canal? We could not tell. And we have never heard anything like it before... or since.)

Thank you, God, that you do abide with us during days when the sun shines and days when we struggle to find the light. This is the first verse of the lovely hymn we heard:

Abide with me; fast falls the eventide;
The darkness deepens; Lord with me abide.
When other helpers fail and comforts flee,
Help of the helpless, O abide with me.'

Someone who abides with us, is someone who lives with us. Not 'stays' with us on a temporary basis, but lives and dwells in the same place as us. This is the kind of God we have: not one who loves us from a distance, but one who lives inside us. As the Genie in Disney's Aladdin puts it, 'Phenomenal cosmic power. Itty bitty living space!'8

You might not be able to see a way through your current pain, but I totally believe that God does. I pray that as you read this, between shouting at my words and crying through your loss, he will bring healing to your broken, damaged heart.

But do you know what? You have to LET him. You have to ask him and you have to let go of your hurt and frustration and anger. Maybe not all in one go, but at least to start to think, 'Maybe, one day' in your heart. OK?

If you know someone who is grieving like this and their grief feels unhealthy and all consuming, don't give up on them. Continue to pray for God to use you to break through into their sorrow. He can do it. In fact, ONLY he can. But he may use you to help.

LESSONS FROM NAOMI

One of the stories in the Bible that has given me a great deal of comfort during my lifetime is the account of Naomi in the book of Ruth. Her personal journey has a great deal to teach us about both grief and about comfort.

1. Grief makes us bitter
This book in the Old Testament describes how Naomi lost her two sons and her husband in a famine. She felt as though God had turned against her.

Naomi wasn't afraid to truly feel her grief and speak out about it. Not only was she in extreme pain, but it is quite clear who she thought was responsible for her loss. We read her saying, 'The Lord's hand has gone out against me!'

Is this how you feel, too? Do you feel as though God has been so harsh to you it is as though his own hand has slapped you in the face? I know a number of people who have shared Naomi's sense of injustice and anguish. She had not yet seen in her own life the truth of Psalm 34:18 that, 'The Lord is near to the broken hearted and saves those who are crushed in spirit.'[9]

'And she said to them, Call me not Naomi [pleasant]; call me Mara [bitter], for the Almighty has dealt very bitterly with me. I went out full, but the Lord has brought me home again empty. Why call me Naomi, since the Lord has testified against me, and the Almighty has afflicted me?"(Ruth 1: 20-21).[10]

Her words and her demeanour show a very depressed, bitter and even angry spirit, don't they?

Perhaps they remind you of someone you know right now.

I was once at a Christian conference in the evening meeting. As part of the team, I was on the stage, but I wasn't 'on duty' that night, so I was just sitting and listening to the speaker. Suddenly a detailed prophetic word began to form in my mind and I started to get that familiar agitated feeling in my heart that I was meant to share it. I asked the man who was leading the event if I could have some 'space' in the meeting. He could see I was shaking and allowed me to whisper the gist of the word to him.

I went to the front of the stage and called out a name. I spoke the name of 'Mara', and in a longer, more detailed word, I said something like:

'There is a lady here called Mara who is full of bitterness. She feels as though God has turned his face away from her and she is cast down. She is unable to reach out to anyone – especially God – and her relationships are in tatters. She has been badly abused and has never dealt with that trauma. Tonight the Lord wants to change your name.'

There was a silence. Nobody moved. Awkward!

I urged that lady to come and get some prayer. The worship band began to play a song. I believe that 13 ladies then very slowly made their way to the front. It may have been 12. It was a bit of a blur. All of them were called Mary or a derivation of that name, or associated themselves somehow with the name 'Mara.'

103

I shall never forget looking at them all in total disbelief. There was a black lady, a stunning young Asian girl in a sari, a white lady with small glasses, a young girl, an old woman... each one so different but all bound by bitterness and grief. The prayer team came forward and we started to pray for these lovely women. Some of their husbands came too, longing for their wives to be set free. One mature older man shared with many tears that he and his wife had never been able to have sex because of a violent rape she had suffered so many years before.

The lady just stood and stared at me saying over and over, 'How did you know my name? How did you know my name?'

Two days later I saw this couple in a shop holding hands and giggling. They looked like they were truly in love again and I had every hope that their relationship would be fully healed. What's more, so did they.

2. Grief alters us

When Naomi got back to Israel, her old friends hardly recognised her. The physical toll of her grief had played itself out in her body and her spirit to such a degree that it had altered her physically. She had huge pain about her past and deep uncertainty about her future.

Is this how you feel too? Do you look at yourself and see a mere shadow of your former self? Do your friends speak and act as though they are deeply concerned about you? And whilst you are grateful for their care, do you actually just feel entirely alone and more than a little bit cross with the normality and happiness of their lives?

Naomi felt something of your journey, too. As have I, and countless others experiencing the rawness of grief. Naomi felt abandoned by God, and she had no reason at this point to think she was wrong to feel that. She did not have the benefit of the 'full stop' at the end of the story of her life, as we do. At this stage, God had not rescued her or met with her or shown himself strong for her. It looked as though he had passed her by. But this is not the God we know.

One of Naomi's daughters-in-law, Ruth, in one of the most touching scenes of the whole Bible, had insisted on returning to Bethlehem with her. So Naomi had been given a companion and one who clearly loved her very deeply and in a very genuine way. They even wept together at the thought of separation. Crying like this demonstrates something really beautiful, but vital: God gives us tears to express our grief. As the wonderful passage from Ecclesiastes reminds us, 'There is . . . a time to weep and a time to laugh, a time to mourn and a time to dance' (Ecclesiastes. 3:1, 4). Tears are an important outlet for our sorrow and one we should not run away from.

3. Grief can mask God's intentions for us

Even though Naomi couldn't see it coming and couldn't have predicted it (even when it was round the corner) God had an intricate plan to meet her needs and restore both her faith and joy.

Think about this for a second. We may be round the corner from the next answer to prayer... but we can't see it. It is still hidden, out of sight and appears to be not even on its way. But that is not a true reflection of what is actually happening! It is just round the corner. None of us can see round corners. We were not built that way.

An old friend of mine was once out for a run. He was praying into a financial need he had at that time. As he ran over the walkway across a busy motorway, a piece of paper fluttered under his running shoe. It was a £50 note. He could not believe that God had provided part of the answer in such a practical and amazing way at a time he was not expecting it at all.

God can actually make something out of nothing. He doesn't need to start with something! He can use an entirely hopeless situation to get us back on track. God took Naomi out of death and famine and led her back to the land where he could bless her. She didn't see it, couldn't fathom it and even blamed God for abandoning her along the way, but that didn't stop him delivering his promises to her.

God has the same kind of plan for you. He does not enjoy your grief and your struggles. In fact, he feels them with you. He wants you to come through them and he wants to get you to a place of blessing again. And, He can handle anything you throw at him in the meantime.

Your healing is around the corner. Start trusting and believing for it today!

4. Grief is part of God's plan

Naomi and Ruth returned to Bethlehem at just the time God planned it – the beginning of harvest. As you may know, there was no welfare state system in those days, but there was a way for the poor to help provide for themselves. Landowners could only harvest the grain in their fields once. Grapes could only be picked from the vines once. Those who were poor were then allowed to 'glean' or take what was left over. And since Ruth was the younger and stronger, she offered: 'Let me go to the fields and pick up the leftover grain behind anyone in whose eyes I find favour.'

> 'And Ruth the Moabite said to Naomi, "Let me go to the field and glean among the ears of grain after him in whose sight I shall find favor." And she said to her, "Go, my daughter."So she set out and went and gleaned in the field after the reapers, and she happened to come to the part of the field belonging to Boaz, who was of the clan of Elimelech. (Ruth 2:2-3).[11]

'As it turned out,' is one of those amazing little phrases. Stamped into those short words are the blessing and favour of God. Do you think he could be at work in your story right now? What could he be setting up on your behalf? What could he turn around for your good? As I once heard the preacher J. John say, 'The more we pray, the more coincidences happen.'

I long for you to have a day when you are no longer fearing the future or wounded by the past, when you can smile and say 'As it turned out, God was FOR me not against me!'

Those short words are of such significance because behind them is the hand of a God who keeps his promises. One of which is to defend 'the cause of the fatherless and the widow, . . . giving them food and clothing' (Deuteronomy 10:18).[12]

Behind every circumstance you are facing right now is the majesty of God. It may not look like it or feel like it, but it is true.

There is nothing that he finds too hard and no circumstance that beats him or reduces his power. His aim for us is to have life in all its abundance and he can use any and every situation to get us there.

God's destiny for Ruth and Naomi was not an endless struggle, and that is not what his desires are for you either. He has a wonderful future planned out for you, but he will not reveal it to you ahead of his perfect (slightly annoying) and sometimes 11th hour, timing. It would be great if God would tell us his dreams for us before they come to pass. But that would mean we would somehow try to engineer them our way, or stop trusting in him to achieve them.

When Naomi went back to Bethlehem, she arrived in a hopeless state of mind. That is often one of the results of bereavement – especially multiple grief. When we grieve, we can see nothing but a bleak and empty future. Life takes on a bitter taste and we can't see a way forward.

What God really wants from each of us is faith in the darkness, trust in the face of questions and hope in a season of natural despair.

The other evening I was at a church curry night and found myself sitting next to a blind lady. She told me that one of the benefits of being blind was that you had to learn to trust others so deeply. She was so excited and inspiring as she shared how trusting her new guide dog, Jessie, mimicked the way she was learning to trust God in the dark.

The darkness of trust can seem to last a while. But it will only continue as long as God needs it to.

I was shocked to hear a Bishop TD Jakes sermon online recently where he said something along these lines - and I paraphrase, 'Do you feel at a standstill in your Christian walk? Are you always struggling with the same issues? Maybe God is keeping you where you are because you haven't yet learnt what you need to learn in order to move on! You haven't graduated yet, so you can't move up a class.'

The sentiment of that really struck an unpleasant but truthful chord in me. I feel as though I lost around six months of my life this past year. I was so full of gloom and was functioning at the lowest possible level in many areas of my life. I wasn't moving forward because I didn't have the capacity to. I had to wait until certain emotions were dealt with and my attitudes were changed.

There is often a wait sown in to the promises of God. Forty years in the desert for the Israelites, Daniel holed up in the lion's den, Joseph stuck in prison, Jonah incarcerated in the stomach of the whale, Jesus in the depths of the tomb. Fulfilment of God's purposes is rarely, if ever, instant.

When Naomi heard whose field Ruth had gleaned in, she responded with great enthusiasm and an immediate apparent return to hope. Look at her language here. It seems like a different woman:

'"The Lord bless him!" Naomi said to her daughter-in-law. "He has not stopped showing his kindness to the living and the dead." She added, "That man is our close relative; he is one of our guardian-redeemers."' (Ruth 2:20).[13]

Had she forgotten this man existed? Could she not have gone to him and told him of her plight in the first place? We don't know... but what is more amazing is that God caused it to be HIS fields that Ruth came across first. Naomi recognises that too. Understanding the kindnesses of God releases us to trust the apparently long silences of heaven.

Boaz was the closest living relative of Elimelech – the man who had been Naomi's husband. The law in Israel stated that when a man died without children, his brother or the closest relative to him, was to marry the widow and have a child with her. That child would belong to the dead man and then come to inherit his property. When Boaz stepped into her life, Naomi's faith was released from its prison of fear. God had not abandoned them after all. He was still good! He could still be trusted! Maybe good things were happening for her again.

RESTORATION

The rest of the book of Ruth is not about death, famine, loss and grief but a wonderful romance. Boaz meets Ruth and marries her.
'So Boaz took Ruth and she became his wife. Then he went to her, and the LORD enabled her to conceive, and she gave birth to a son...'

Naomi is given true hope again.

'So Boaz took Ruth and she became his wife. When he made love to her, the Lord enabled her to conceive, and she gave birth to a son... Then Naomi took the child in her arms and cared for him.' (Ruth 4:13, 16).[14]

As far as we know, Ruth had been childless all the time she had been married to Mahlon. Now the Lord had given her a son. Naomi finally had a grandson, even though he was not strictly in her own actual bloodline from her husband or children. More than this, Naomi's old age was secure and her future was safe. God had not left her in the lurch after all.

In fact, he had arranged all of the tiny seemingly insignificant details of her painful life to restore her and provide for her. And though she didn't live to see it, the Bible tells us that Obed became the ancestor of King David and ultimately of Jesus himself.

What Naomi and Ruth experienced in the restoration of their happiness was far more than they ever lost.

You may feel as though you have lost everything. You may have lost your wife, or your daughter, or your friend, or your job, or your home, or all of these things. Even then, even in the midst of that loss and that pain ALL IS NOT LOST. Why?

Because God never stops working on your behalf.

Ever.

RECONSTRUCTIVE SURGERY
LOSING YOURSELF

And you do come out of it, that's true. After a year, after five. But you don't come out of it like a train coming out of a tunnel, bursting through the downs into sunshine and that swift, rattling descent to the Channel; you come out of it as a gull comes out of an oil-slick.'

Julian Barnes[1]

Life can take us by surprise. It can shake us to the core, and kick us mercilessly in the teeth. It feels far from kind and easy at times.

Unexpectedly losing your health is frightening and exhausting. Not just for you, but also for those left trying to care for you.

There are many reasons that a person's health suddenly changes. Perhaps a loss of memory after an accident, problems with mental health after a bereavement, or a new battle with clinical depression following an illness or change in circumstance.

This section of the book talks about one couple's experiences with some of those issues.

But God does not want us to stand still. Sometimes he takes us a long way out of our comfort zone. Sometimes he allows us to walk through dark valleys in order to help us rely on him more fully.

I am about to tell you a true story in the words of those who lived it. I feel an immense sense of privilege as I do so, for their account is a wonderful and amazing one. Thank you to Andy and Michele Hawthorne.[3]

But first, a story.

ANDY'S JOURNAL
BANGKOK 2012

The tribe finally settled in a new land at the end of the summer, far away from where they set out from months before. Scouts had been sent ahead to select the right location. None they passed through seemed perfect, but with winter approaching a decision had to be made. That first winter was difficult for every member of the tribe. Food was scarce and the reserves from the summer's hunting, that which could be carried, soon ran out.

In those first few years there was much to challenge them and much to learn. Migration routes of the local wildlife were discovered, providing a reliable source of meat; the best fishing sites were found through trial and error; the forests were scoured for any food above and below ground. Nothing in life was easy but the tribe was happy, absorbed and united in overcoming the trials of surviving.

With sources of sustainable food guaranteed, the tribe turned their attention to devising more timesaving and technologically refined ways of improving their existence. As the decade became two, the people grew increasingly comfortable as the challenges of their new territory faded. With this came the growth of boredom amongst the tribe; conflicts broke out more frequently and ill health increased. A full generation on from their arrival at the new location the elders of the tribe, weighing up the situation decided it was time to move again.

The wisdom of these elders was to know when the time was right to change direction; to journey into unfamiliar territory. They recognized that their well-stocked and established home had become exhausted of treasure in ways more subtle, but just as threatening to their happiness, as if the land had been stripped bare and the rivers drained. What lay ahead out of sight around the corner would challenge them, but it would enrich them much more than standing still.[2]

LOSING FACE

Michele and I had a really fruitful time out in Australia. At a conference
we attended there an inspirational missionary shared about his work in
the slums of Manila. He spoke about the fact that some Christians have a
terrible time with all sorts of awful tragedies happening in their lives – he
shared about his own 25-year-battle with depression for example – whilst
other believers seem to live a charmed, easy existence.

Michele and I looked at each other. We didn't know what it was to suffer,
not really. We were those kind of people and we felt very blessed by God.

After Australia, we had arranged, with the help of a kind business supporter,
for a stopover on our way home for the weekend in the beautiful Mandarin
Oriental Hotel on the Chao Phraya River. Before we enjoyed the wonderful
facilities however, we were to be exposed to a very different face of Bangkok.

Ash and Anj Barker are an Australian couple who founded the 'Surrender
Conference', which was one of the places at which I had been invited to
speak. For the last 10 years this couple have lived, worked and served Jesus
among the very poor who live in the Klong Toey slum. During 'Surrender'
I had arranged to visit them, and so, on our first morning in Bangkok, we
took a hair-raising ride on a motorbike taxi, right into the heart of the slum.

Like most of the Aussies we've met, Ash and Anj are the most down-to-
earth couple, but they're also one of the most incredible. They live in the
toughest bit of the Klong Toey slum, with gangs dealing drugs, prostitution,
and the constant threat of violent recriminations on their own doorstep.
In this context, they have brought up their three kids and consistently
blessed the community through a school, a church plant and various
business enterprises. We were both completely blown away by these
amazing people.

One of their businesses is called 'Cooking with Pooh' – a Thai cookery
school in the heart of the slum run by the eponymous Pooh. Amazingly
it was rated as the number one thing to do in Bangkok on Trip Advisor
(number two is visiting the Grand Palace) and it has launched a cook book
that was featured on The Jonathan Ross Show in the UK. Anyway, we were
privileged to have the pleasure of the famous Pooh cooking our lunch
at her school.

After an incredibly slow journey back to our hotel through the snarled-up traffic that blights every one of the world's mega cities, we made our way to the oasis of calm that is the Mandarin Oriental. We spent the late afternoon swimming and relaxing and booked a riverboat cruise and a lovely looking Thai restaurant across the river for later that evening.

At 8.30pm we got the river taxi across to the restaurant and sat down to order our food.

Michele said she wanted to go to the toilet and I sat sipping a glass of wine, without a care in the world.

She walked round a little bend...

Suddenly there was a major commotion by the toilets and an American guy ran out saying 'Who's with the blonde woman in the black dress?' I jumped up and ran to the lobby to find Michele lying unconscious in a pool of blood, with a huge open gash on her cheek. As I moved towards her she came round but was obviously in terrible pain and was mumbling and moaning incoherently.

Had she had a fit and fallen? Had someone attacked with a baseball bat? There was nobody around to see or ask. I didn't know. Somehow she had lost consciousness and fallen hard, so hard onto that marble floor that her face was totally smashed in. I caught a glimpse of one of the huge pillars with a hard-edged ornate plinth at the bottom and wondered if this was what had cut her so badly. I stared back at Michele, my beautiful wife, now so disfigured and covered in blood.

Someone brought some ice and we tried to cool her down. Then a doctor came along from somewhere, and said, 'You need to get her in a taxi and take her to the hospital, right now!'

The taxi ride through the grinding traffic seemed to take forever. It was horrendous. Michele was flailing around in the back with me.

Suddenly I noticed blood starting to come out of her ear on the other side of her face and also her nose. I didn't know what to do. It was terrible!

When we finally got her to Casualty, they rushed her straight through and immediately did a brain scan. The neurologist said he thought there was bleeding on the brain and that there were definitely multiple fractures to her face.

I sat there reeling, resigning myself to the fact that I would now be a carer, looking after a brain-damaged wife for the rest of my life. I didn't ever think she was going to die. But I couldn't believe that I was ever going to get my wife back. Not the Michele I knew anyway.

Two days after being reminded of our 'charmed existence' we were suddenly living a terrifying one.

At this point the nursing staff asked my permission to restrain her because Michele was so agitated and was trying to pull her various tubes out. This involved tying her to the bed with cords. It honestly looked like medieval torture to me and I found it deeply disturbing. The following day, struggling to treat her, they asked if they could do it again. This time I said 'no' and promised I would stay right by her bed and do all I could to keep her calm and stop her hurting herself.

I didn't trust the people at the hospital. Hardly any of them could speak any English and I knew none of their language. We had come through the part of the hospital being refurbished and the whole place looked like a dump to me. I felt totally and utterly desperate. I was unsure that Michele would be safe and I could do nothing about it.

I wanted to stay the night with her in Intensive Care but the doctor said I had to leave and so, dejectedly, I went back to my hotel room around 1.30am for a sleepless night, wondering if our lives would ever be the same again.

I fell into a fitful sleep and was awoken in the middle of the night by Michele's voice screaming my name, 'ANDY!', in a terribly pained and anguish-filled voice. Nothing like that has ever happened to me before. It was a horribly dark nightmare but it felt so real. I was totally freaked out and jumped out of my skin. I rang the hospital for an update. Nothing had changed.

I phoned a few friends and asked them to start praying and thus started the amazing viral outpouring of love and prayer that made such a difference in those first few traumatic days.

James Aladrian, our Message prayer team leader was one of the first people who Collette Dallas, one of my team contacted. His text was the first of thousands of encouraging texts, emails and Facebook posts that kept us going. (How did people cope before this stuff?)

His text went like this, 'We were praying just before Collette told me what happened. I was meditating on this scripture and I just didn't feel it was a coincidence. As I was meditating, Collette called me. The scripture is Psalm 40: 'O God the Lord, The strength of my salvation, You have covered (sheltered) my head in the day of battle.' God is with Michele! His hand is on her head! We are praying! James.'

Saturday March 31st 2012

I left the hotel for the hospital, fearful about what I would face, yet
determined to be strong for Michele. She was completely disorientated
and, disturbingly, very anxious when I arrived. The slightest touch from
the nursing staff and she would scream the place down.

The whole day was punctuated with screams of, 'Stop it, stop it, it hurts!'
and 'No!' as Michele wrestled around on her bed with sometimes up to
eight staff trying to get her drip in or give her some medication. It sounds
a bit dramatic but every time it happened, it was like a dagger to my heart.
I want you to understand that Michele is the most stoical woman you could
imagine. She doesn't scream or shout when she is in pain; she is quiet and
breathes deeply. To see her shouting out in such a vulnerable and child-like
way was heartrending. I felt both utterly wretched and helpless.

First thing, I went with her to the CAT scan area to check again for bleeding
on the brain.

Incredibly there was now no sign of it. 'Was this a miracle?' I thought.
The neurosurgeon even said he thought she would settle down and that if
all went well we could leave the hospital in a few days, but first we would
have to see the plastic surgeon, Dr Patel, to see what he thought of all the
broken bones in her face.

Dr Patel grew on me a lot but he did have a strange habit of giving you the
worst news you could possibly imagine with a satisfied grin on his face.
The news on this occasion was that Michele definitely needed reconstructive
surgery on the five different breaks in her face and would also need to have
titanium plates fitted and her jaw wired up for four to six weeks.

I was shocked and initially thought, who is this grinning buffoon, in a
foreign hospital who wants to reconstruct my wife's face? At this point
I didn't realise (as I had come through the back entrance) that BNH is
actually a very smart, modern facility that specialises in cosmetic surgery
and that Dr Patel is a top plastic surgeon. I asked if there was any way
Michele could go home and have the surgery done in England but he
assured me it was not possible. That was another shock. They also said we
would have to wait for the brain to settle down a bit before any surgery.

They took Michele to Intensive Care where she again writhed around, pulling at her wires, screaming if anyone touched her. It was horrendous. I read the news that people were posting about Michele on Facebook and that Ivy (our home church in Manchester) had called an emergency prayer meeting. The lifeline of encouraging texts, emails and Facebook posts well and truly kicked in.

I knew lots of people were praying, but to be honest I felt totally bereft and abandoned by God – a new and very disturbing feeling for me. It does all sound a bit much writing it down, but at this point I felt like I was cracking up so much so that when the insurance company phoned and asked me how I was doing, I started sobbing uncontrollably.

In my adult life, I have probably only really cried three or four times but on Saturday 31 March, I probably wept more than a dozen times. What was worse, I would sit in the corner of the Intensive Care room sobbing and Michele wouldn't even notice. She really was in an anxious, disturbed, disorientated world all of her own.

Just at my lowest ebb on Saturday evening, four people turned up at the same time; four people who in different ways were such a blessing to me over those difficult days. It was Anj and Ash Barker, who we had met on Friday, and Peter and Ineke Cook, who are leaders of Christ Church Bangkok, the church that stands literally next door to the hospital. Peter and Ineke had heard through a friend about what had happened and insisted that I should stay at their lovely vicarage next door. It really was a Godsend, so I was able to cancel the scruffy soulless guesthouse I had booked to stay in by the hospital.

Also just what I needed was Ash and Anj who saw the state I was in and took me out for two pints of beer and a Thai curry. They are fantastic people and every day it was great to get to know them a little better. Every time they seemed to have a new story of criminal activity and scary violence right outside their slum, yet seemed to be able to tell the stories with a twinkle in their eyes and the love of Jesus in their hearts.

So to bed – this time at Christ Church Vicarage – for a night of interrupted sleep, mainly because my phone was constantly buzzing with texts affirming love, concern and prayers from every corner of the globe.

The next day was another day in Intensive Care with my beautiful wife with the broken face. It started with a real shocker from the surgeon who was due to operate on her on Monday. He said he thought she would need a tracheotomy so she could continue to breathe while her chin and her nose were being fixed. This of course would mean she wouldn't be able to speak for at least a week. Our kids were on their way out to see us. I couldn't bear the thought of her not being able to talk to them, not after all she had been through. It was another complete kick in the teeth and I think because I appeared so shocked he said he would go and have another look at the X-ray.

I think something rose up in me and I said 'No more!' and for the next hour until he came back, I prayed in English and in tongues and said 'Lord, please not this as well!' Mr (smiley) Patel came back and said actually he had decided the nose was OK, and we didn't need a tracheotomy after all. I was so relieved and for the first time, thankful.

Peter and his wife Ineke then arrived with anointing oil and we had a special time praying over Michele and anointing her. By now she was much calmer and even said 'Amen' after the prayer – the first sane and measured response I'd had from her in almost 48 hours.

I slipped out to find some food while Michele was sleeping and ended up in an Irish bar in Thailand eating Sunday lunch – Michele would have been appalled! It was hard not to notice the number of overweight, pasty Englishmen accompanied by gorgeous, scantily clad Thai girls. I had stumbled on the edges of a very seedy side of Bangkok life. Ash would later tell me that there is a full-blown sex tourism industry that specialises in ripping off wealthy Westerners who know they are getting scammed but can't resist. It costs £8 for an hour. People go in and make these girls do whatever they want. It's everywhere.

Meanwhile the Body of Christ began to get moving and the worldwide prayer for Michele really started to heat up. I also experienced his love through his people in Bangkok. The legendary John and Gillian Robinson turned up and we had another special time of prayer. John also agreed to meet me in the vicarage the following morning for prayer during the operation. But still I went to bed that night full of fear.

At 12.30am I received a call from my son, Sam. He and Beth were coming out to join us but there had obviously been some mess up booking flights, as to everyone's surprise the flights had been booked from Birmingham and they were supposed to fly at 6.30am that morning.

The next hour was spent sorting things out and finding them flights from Manchester the following day for £300 cheaper. Perhaps it was good because for a short while it helped me to take my mind off what was going on.

Then at 2.30am, I got a call from Thimothee, a pastor we have supported in Haiti, who had heard about Michele's accident and phoned to say they were praying for her there, too. He said something that made more sense than ever before: 'We have to suffer, brother, but God will hold your hand through it'. At this stage, to be honest, I don't think I felt anyone holding my hand, just a real sense of fear for my wife and for the future.

THE DAY OF THE OPERATION, 8AM

I'm hoping that writing this one hour before Michele is taken down to surgery, will be cathartic because right now I feel as low as I ever have in my whole life. I thought Saturday was bad, but as thousands of people are praying for me in literally every corner of the globe, all I feel is despair. Torturous questions haunted me all night about just what Michele will be like once all this is over. Will I ever get my sparky amazing wife back or someone very different? I'm up for being the best husband I can be whatever happens but the thoughts are killing me.

It wasn't helped by me making my way to the hospital at 6.30am and having the following 'conversation':

'How are you, Shelley?'
'...OK.'
'You're in Bangkok.'
'...Am I?'
'Where do you live?'
'...I don't know.'
'Do you remember Australia?'
'...No.'

She's forgotten so much right now and once again doesn't even notice me sobbing in the corner of her room. I know it's ridiculous for a guy who never cries, but I just can't stop. What has happened to me?

I suddenly had a flap about just what happens if she is sick due to the anaesthetic and her jaw is wired up. But the doctors have slightly put my mind at rest on that. I'm also plagued by thoughts, 'How on earth could this have happened? Why didn't she put her hands out to stop her fall?' 'How can a fall cause so much damage to her face and rattle her brain so much that she is the way she is right now?'

BEFORE THE OPERATION

The surgeon has just come in and just when I'm wondering will Michele ever be the same again, he has the best conversation with her that anyone has had since she arrived in the Intensive Care unit. Maybe it's a blessing with the battering she's about to take that she is not really aware what's going on and is so exhausted that as soon as they have prodded and poked her, she is straight back to sleep.

The surgeon just said it could be up to three months for her brain to fully recover but she is doing well and that we could expect that recovery. I have also received a phone call again from a lady called Jane who works at Christ Church next door. Her adopted daughter, Noi, is one of the nurses on the unit and is a Christian.

As we travelled down to the operating theatre, I spoke to Michele who appeared unbelievably calm and accepting (I honestly wasn't sure if it was the brain injury or the peace of Jesus), and left for the prayer meeting at Christ Church, once again feeling a little bit uncomfortable. Fortunately, my phone buzzed with a text from our lovely Collette Dallas:

'I really sense that Michele is experiencing the Lord's peace now and when she wakes up she will testify of a wonderful encounter with Him on the operating table.' Amen.

AFTER THE PRAYER MEETING

There were six of us at the Christ Church prayer meeting including John Robinson, as the texts came in from the 2.30am meeting in Manchester and the precious brothers and sisters in Uganda who were praying and fasting. I can only say that it felt that we were at the epicentre of something God was coordinating. At around 1:00am, I received a text from John Bunjo in Uganda saying he felt they had been given an encouraging spiritual 'breakthrough'.

Facebook has been such a massive lifeline. I have not been able to do anything else but read it. The total outpouring of love and the hundreds of messages on there are my fuel. I am so moved by them. I feel so vulnerable and yet I know that all around the world 50,000+ people are praying. Whole movements of people are praying. It's very humbling.

I'm now sitting in Intensive Care waiting for her return and wondering just what she looks like right now and what she will look like into the future.

AFTER THE OPERATION

After almost four hours she returned and I was faced with perhaps the most traumatic hour of the whole time here – and that really is saying something. They were worried that because she was so shattered and confused this morning, she wouldn't be able to breathe properly and so placed a tube up her nose and into her throat to help her to breathe. The only problem was that it was driving Michele crazy. It was massively uncomfortable and at one point blood was coming out of her nose and mouth as she fought to breathe.

I had to get the anaesthetist back and convince her to remove the offending tube. (I told this story to a nurse friend here and she laughed and said that in the NHS if you made 'clinical suggestions' to them like this, they would tell you to sling your hook!) But this woman responded to my urgent shouts 'Be quick! Be quick' and pulled out the tube, at which point, Michele settled right down and it was almost like suddenly she had many of her faculties back.

I do wonder if, on the back of all the many prayers that were lifted up for Michele, we did indeed have the breakthrough and her brain had received a major kick-start of healing from the Holy Spirit.

Suddenly, she wanted to see Sam and Beth, her mum, her friend Gail and even asked for a cup of tea. Talk about a different woman from the one that went in for the operation – it was amazing! Despite this, she was obviously in a lot of pain from the surgery and halfway through the afternoon, after a really special time with her showing some of the hundreds of texts and emails that have arrived from all around the world, she was dosed up on painkillers and has slept ever since. A chapter of one of my books has the title 'Life is a rollercoaster'. Never was this more true for me than April 2, 2012.

Once again, Ash, who I have now officially decided is one of the nicest people I have ever met, and a rampant Manchester United fan in to the bargain, came round and took me out for a beer and a chicken tikka masala. Wrong in Thailand I know, but again, just what was needed at the time.

After six days in intensive care they took her down to a normal ward where I could sleep on the sofa. Sam and Beth, our kids, had come. Michele was able to recognise them but her short-term memory was worse than a goldfish with dementia.

'Andy, I can't open my mouth.'
'You've had an accident love'
A few minutes later,
'Andy, I can't open my mouth.'
'I know Shelley. You've had a fall.'

Was this like the proof of some kind of lasting brain damage? I was frightened I would end up living with a basket case and everyone would stop praying and get on with their lives.

ONE WEEK LATER

It is now a week since the operation. Michele has very little short-term memory and is still often confused. Her eye socket in particular looks a mess and having her jaw wired up is massively frustrating. But I am actually starting to 'see the wood from the trees' and realise already how much worse things could have been and how much God has sustained us both through the most difficult 10 days of our lives.

Firstly, the hospital, which seemed shabby when we were first admitted (due to the fact that we were whisked in a side door) has actually been amazing. The facilities and the level of care from nursing staff despite the language barrier have been nothing short of outstanding. It struck me that perhaps if this accident was going to happen anywhere apart from Manchester, Bangkok might be the place, especially for a hospital that specialises in cosmetic surgery, often of the 'lady-boy' variety. I didn't realise at the time, but this is one of the hospitals rich Americans go on 'holiday' to have their cosmetic surgery done.

Secondly, Sam and Beth being able to join us has been such a blessing for Michele, and I know that we have been knitted together as a family through this trauma. I'm sure that it has been significant for them to once again be exposed to ministry amongst the poor through Ash and Anj. Both of them are now saying that they would love to work here in the future in some capacity.

Thirdly, the worldwide prayer from literally dozens of nations has been quite something. Thousands of people who have never met Michele or me have been fasting and praying. All over the planet. It's been a viral prayer movement that I believe will bless the people who were part of it and ultimately, me, Michele and our family and the things we are involved in more ways than I can imagine right now.

Lastly, we haven't seen the dramatic healing that I hoped for, nor have we been spared from trauma, but as I look back I can see definite moments where God intervened. As Michele lay on the bed, writhing and moaning with blood starting to drip from her ear and nose, all the signs were of bleeding on the brain, and initially that's what the scan suggested too. We cried out to God and the next scan gave the all clear.

I was definitely told she had a broken nose along with all the other injuries. This would have meant a tracheotomy again. I prayed in desperation and, as far as I could tell, the break had gone.

Even this week we've had to look to the Lord so many times. Her leg and a lot of her right side went numb. Occasionally, after lucid moments, she suddenly talks complete nonsense and yet each time I pray and do receive peace after the initial anxiety.

We've been reading The Word for Today together and the last two days have seemed particularly pertinent. Yesterday's reading (Easter Day) said, 'Bring your wounds to Jesus and let him heal your body, mind and soul'. Today's said, 'When you stop struggling with the when's, where's, why's and how's, you start experiencing God's peace in a way you never have before'.

That's what I long for with Michele right now – God's healing and peace as we move into the future. In one sense it seems uncertain but it is actually built on God's sure and certain blessing on our lives – and a massive foundation of prayer.

Two things came through at our Bangkok prayer meeting that I also think will be significant. Firstly, we are entering a season where we are about to learn what it's like to not just minister, but be ministered to; and, secondly, there are some things that I can't control, much as I would love to – but God really is in control.

Those two lessons, I think, will have a profound impact on whatever we do in the future.'

ONE YEAR ON

I caught up with Andy and Michele recently to ask them how they were now.

For the two weeks after the accident Michele recalls nothing at all.

'It is strange not to be able to remember most of three weeks of your life, especially three such significant ones for my health. But I think I am grateful that I don't recall much. It sounded a total nightmare for Andy to live through and whilst I am sad he felt so isolated in it, I obviously couldn't have been in any way a comfort to him.'

I asked Andy if he felt it was a blessing that she couldn't recall the horrors he had witnessed. 'Oh completely!' he replied. 'It was great that God has cushioned her from that. It was awful watching it, but it would have been terrible for her to re-live any of it.'

Michele spoke again, 'I am an artist. How things look is very important to me. I am a visual person. Having my face reconstructed was terrifying. I didn't know what I would look like. Would I be ugly, disfigured and 'difficult' for other people to look at? Would I still look like me? These were questions I really had to face. But of course, Andy had faced them all in the hospital. My realisations were much later, weeks later really.'

'It is incredible when you think that my eye socket, my cheek, my jaw and my chin were all smashed in and I had a big open gash on the side of my face for three days and that now, you can hardly tell.'

I inspected Michele's face at close quarters and looked at a picture of her at the time of her injury. It looked like a different person. But it was little over a year later.

'It turns out that the man who did my surgery was one of the best plastic surgeons out there. You just can't see his stitches.'

I agreed. You can't.

'Can you remember anything at all?' I asked.

'I do have a few short but distinct memories of my time in hospital after the kids arrived. But then again, I am not sure if this is because they have told me things... I don't think so. One day Beth took me out in the wheelchair into a pretty courtyard garden in the middle of the hospital. It was roasting outside without the air conditioning. I remember being terrified of the automatic doors. I kept thinking they were going to close on me. It was an irrational fear but it was very real. It was totally unlike me to be so panicky about something as mundane as that.'

'Another time, the electric bed I was lying on suddenly went wrong and I sort of began to disappear in the middle. Beth said it looked as though the bed was trying to eat me alive! She ran to get a nurse and was told they couldn't come straight away. She kicked up such a fuss and insisted it got sorted NOW. I was so proud of her for sticking up for me!'

'For a while I could only be fed liquids through a straw. One thing they gave me was a protein drink made from processed Thai rice. It sounds strange, but I really liked the flavour of it. It made the experience of being liquid-fed not quite so awful. I doubt they'd have given me that on the NHS!'

'One day the Hardy family who are at our church in Manchester were in Thailand on a mission visit and came to see us. I remember John, their young boy who has had a number of serious brain operations counselling and reassuring me. It was amazing. His maturity, trust and faith because of what he has gone through were so inspiring.'

'I know now that my questions and comments to Andy and the kids were repetitive. Apparently I kept asking questions like: "Does my Mum know?" "Does Gail know?" To which Andy would respond that they did, of course.'

'One day I said, 'Does that Collette who works for you know?'

'It seemed as though some deeper parts of my memory were returning.'

'Incidentally, Collette, who is the person in question, was made up to make my top three!'

'Obviously you have heard that there were times in the hospital where I was in huge trauma and distress. Thankfully I don't recall those days. I am actually able to remember moments where I was really peaceful. One day my daughter Beth was stroking my hair. There was some chilled music on. Apparently I said, "It doesn't get much better than this. This is fabulous!"'

'I think I knew that having all my family around me was such a blessing.'

'One night when Andy had been asleep on the sofa he got up to go to the loo. I said: "Andy you look dead fit. You look 12!" Then he knew I was brain damaged! Ha ha!'

'I used the word "fabulous" a lot. And that's not an easy word to say when your jaw is wired together! I must have sounded like a talentless and rather drunk ventriloquist!'

I asked her how she was feeling now, all those months later.

'In one minute of our lives we went from elation to despair. My health and well-being were taken in an instant. That takes some time to come to terms with.'

'For five months after the accident I was on some kind of spiritual high. I had had so much prayer, protection and a deep measure of emotional and physical healing. I felt so cushioned. I was joyful and overwhelmingly grateful to God.'

'I think my respect and love for Andy just soared too. As I thought back over all he went through for me I couldn't fathom it. It was incredible. I know he says he didn't have a choice, but he did. He could have cracked up. But he just got on with caring for me, in whatever way was needed.'

'But then, without much warning, this feeling of elation and protection just left me.'

'During my recovery time, Andy was around a great deal. I wasn't able to cook, clean or do any simple tasks. I was totally dependent on others to help me in every way. I had no responsibilities at all.'

'There was a constant stream of people and I loved having visitors. But for some reason I was scared to see people on my own. I am such a sociable person, but I totally lost my confidence in that area. It felt like I couldn't handle crowds anymore. I couldn't even handle couples for long. I felt overwhelmed by the smallest thing.'

'Andy didn't do any meetings for six weeks after we got home and was around the house just being with me and helping out, and that was lovely, but when he started to go back to work a bit and arrange business things again properly, something inside me panicked.'

'I also felt a huge sense of disappointment. So many people had prayed for either a dramatic or a total healing in me. I felt I hadn't delivered either. Was it because my faith was too shallow, or because I wasn't able to trust God for my future? I started to feel very negative about myself.'

'I wanted to tell people I had been restored completely, but it wasn't true. My face was still numb and what's more my heart was, too.'

'People kept saying how marvellous I looked, but I just didn't feel it on the inside.'

'I am not the kind of person who 'does' depression. I just thought I would never have anything like that. I am a fighter and I don't take life lying down. I don't like the label or stigma attached to being a depressed person.'

'I don't think I realised it but I was grieving for what I had been through and for what I had lost. In some ways, I still am.'

'I started getting a lot of offers to run my art workshops again and I thought I might be able to handle it. So I agreed to do a few... but it was taking me hours to prepare something that would have taken minutes before. It was as though my mind couldn't focus or function on what I was asking it to do. Even short tasks took me a long time and I felt as though they weren't up to my standard when they were finished. I felt exhausted and emotionally drained. I had huge waves of self-doubt that lasted days.'

'I really felt I couldn't handle life. I was so down about myself. I looked in the mirror and felt I had let everyone down. I felt a fraud and a failure. All these people had wasted time praying for ME. What was it all for?'

'At my lowest moments I began to wonder if everyone would be better off if I wasn't around. I felt like I was dragging Andy and the family down. At times I struggled with guilt because of how I was feeling too. Should a Christian really experience these kinds of feelings?'

'God brought about a small but significant rescue in terms of my work. I truly wasn't able to handle the various art projects of work that had come in, but I had already said yes to them. One by one, without any reference to one another and for very different reasons, they all fell through. I was so grateful and so relieved. I realised that I was not "better". I needed to stop trying to be and just let myself recover at the pace I needed to. Hard though that was.'

'Just because I looked better on the outside did not mean I was healed on the inside. In fact, I was far from it.'

'One of the things I really grieved was that I couldn't cook. I had always prided myself on catering at the drop of a hat for anybody – small and big parties were fun and not stressful for me. I was known for it. But suddenly, I couldn't boil an egg. It was so humbling and so hard. For a sociable woman who loves to be hospitable, those two things were just gone.'

'I remember trying to cook at Christmas, as I had every other year. The kids were coming home from travelling and like every mum I just wanted to make it special. But it was awful. My head couldn't cope with the many tasks. My mind could only do one thing at a time – and to a different standard than what I was used to. I'm sure to other people this would not have been a big deal, but when it is part of your identity, it is so hard to come to terms with.'

'One evening, I went to an Ivy mission partners event at church. I remember feeling so down and almost not going. No one prayed for me and nothing was said directly to me about how I was feeling but that night the darkness seemed to lift and since then I have been able to cope more.'

LAMENTATIONS 3:22

BECAUSE OF THE LORD'S GREAT LOVE WE ARE NOT CONSUMED,

FOR HIS COMPASSIONS NEVER FAIL

(Maybe just hearing stories about what God was doing across the world just unlocked something spiritual in Michele?)

'I am still struggling with my mind functionality. I cannot multi-task and have to try and focus on one thing at a time to get anything done. I also feel as though I have issues with my memory. People say that's normal for someone in their 50's but I know it has changed beyond just my age. It is definitely a "leftover" from my accident.'

'I was really blessed to talk to a guy at church who had suffered from a head injury. He told me that he had issues for a long time with his memory, personal organisation and functions and that he couldn't work for a while afterwards. I felt pleased that I wasn't the only one.'

'Now I can work again, but only one day a week. I run an art workshop for people to help build their self-esteem. And I am just starting to get my confidence back in the kitchen. I still don't attempt anything too dramatic, but I am glad that I can make a meal now.'

'As to what I have learnt, obviously this has been a massive journey for me. I think I am much more compassionate towards others now, especially those suffering with depression or self doubt. I have a new empathy for that. I don't always know what to say, but I do know how to listen. I never had that kind of patience or sensitivity before. I don't feel I have to work hard to get onto their level. I just am. I know what it is to be that low. It wasn't long ago I was there and I don't have to work hard to remember it.'

'One of the most helpful pieces of writing I have read has been Dennis Wrigley's book on depression, *From Darkness into Light*. It is a set of poems with some beautiful artwork by Christine Garwood. I had never read something that seemed to echo my emotions so faithfully. I would really recommend that for anyone facing any kind of dark cloud in their life.'

'I am doing so much better now. I feel stronger and more able to look forward. Life is for living and I know the truth that God wants me to live it to the full.'

Michele and Andy have come through the hardest challenge they have ever faced, stronger and more aware of God's heart for them. They can sense his hand through every part of the story. Their journey is one of quiet victory, grace and reality. They do not deny the dark and frightening facets of their experience but they know the unequivocal truth that God never left them to face any aspect of it alone.

> 'I remember my affliction and my wandering,
> the bitterness and the gall
> I well remember them, and my soul
> is downcast within me
> Yet this I call to mind and therefore I have hope:
> Because of the Lord's great love we are not consumed,
> for his compassions never fail.
> They are new every morning; great is your faithfulness.
> I say to myself, 'The Lord is my portion;
> therefore I will wait for him.'
> The Lord is good to those whose hope
> is in him, to the one who seeks him;
> It is good to wait quietly for the salvation of the Lord.'
>
> Lamentations 3: 19–26[7]

IDEAL HOME

What Michele went through is obviously hugely unusual and traumatic, but the emotions she has faced since are ones that many people share.

I think it is true to say that I have never met anyone I deeply respect, who has not suffered in some way. The older I get, the more people I meet who God has allowed to be broken. As I have said in earlier chapters, I don't believe that this is some kind of cruel fascination on His part – making trouble or allowing suffering to somehow spite us and 'teach us a lesson.' On the contrary, I am learning that it is about how He works to build us up and move us on.

C.S. Lewis puts it very helpfully in his book, *Mere Christianity*:

> *'Imagine yourself as a living house. God comes in to rebuild that house. At first, perhaps, you can understand what He is doing. He is getting the drains right and stopping the leaks in the roof and so on; you knew that those jobs needed doing and so you are not surprised. But presently he starts knocking the house about in a way that hurts abominably and does not seem to make any sense. What on earth is he up to? The explanation is that he is building quite a different house from the one you thought of – throwing out a new wing here, putting on an extra floor there, running up towers, making courtyards. You thought you were being made into a decent little cottage: but he is building a palace. He intends to come and live in it himself.'*[8]

What kind of dwelling place for God are you?

If I am honest, I am often not a very good one.

I don't have the perfect model figure, unless you are talking about modelling for the Viking catalogue (I have always looked good behind a desk). But I am learning to celebrate the curves and the fleshy, wobbly bits of myself... perhaps a little more than I have before. I haven't got to the stage where they don't matter to me at all but I am journeying towards that day of freedom. (Not nudity you understand. That is for Germans... and the partially sighted.) But true freedom from worrying about that kind of rubbish.

Put it this way, there is plenty of room for God in my ample body.

I try to look nice and keep myself neat and tidy. But I am not obsessive about my mascara or lip gloss. I put makeup on once a day and if it is rude enough to fall off then so be it. There is not enough time in my day to 'RE-APPLY'. Reapplying is for girls and I am not a girl. I am a mature woman with precious little time and energy, four kids and a lot of dishwasher cycles in any given day. So time must be used wisely.

Let me tell you how I see it.

I am a woman. Fact.

I am getting older. Also... fact.

My body grows unsightly, surprisingly strong hair overnight for no apparent purpose other than to test the strength of my poor tweezers. Sadly, fact.

Exercise of any duration and type hurts me. Fact.

Cake is my friend... and yet also my enemy. Fact.

But I don't actually think any of that is a massive priority for God. He wants me to be well and healthy, but he has other things on his heart for me, too. Things much deeper than what others can see of me.

He wants to live IN me, not with me or near me. But actually inside. This means He might need to do some drastic work on me to allow him maximum room.

A house can look amazing until you stay the night. Then you notice the cold draughts coming in at the windows, the loud neighbours, noisy road and leaking shower. It is when you live somewhere that you truly know these things about where you are staying.

You and I are God's dwelling place. He LIVES in US. So what are we like to live in? What kind of house have you made for God? Are you an ideal home?

I know I am not!

The reason God cares more about what we are like inside is because He gets to see it close up. It is where he hangs out. Perhaps you and I need to focus on doing some interior design? And perhaps a little decluttering?

Let's face it, there are many parts of our inner being that are far from pretty aren't there?

Reapplying internal paintwork won't work. God isn't impressed with a lick of gloss-eggshell–matt-white- sheen here and there. He doesn't like fake faith, trite testimonies or superficial smiles. He is not won over by winning words, posh prayers or generous gestures – not if they aren't coming from the heart.

He wants real-deal-true-you purity.

I have SUCH a long way to go before anyone would call me an ideal home for God. But that is my aim. And I know it is His desire for me too.

I totally believe that what Andy and Michele have gone through, and what others suffer with is not pointless and without purpose. I think it is God's way of turning awful into awesome and darkness into light.

Maybe in some ways God is like the smiling Mr Patel? Knowing we need reconstructive surgery and being fully confident of his ability to deliver it.

THE LION'S DEN

THE DEATH OF A CHILD

'The grief that took me out at the knees and that changed my life for ever... was on July 29, 2010 when my placenta erupted at five and a half months pregnancy and I haemorrhaged. My son Benjamin died. As I held his tiny, perfect ten inch body later that day and felt the weight of one pound one ounce on my chest I vowed that I would learn every single lesson that this grief had to teach me, because I never wanted to go through it again.'

Alana Sheeren[1]

I have never lost a child and I can't pretend to fully understand or feel the depth of sorrow that accompanies such a trauma. I am grateful to those who have shared their journey and feelings with me on such a difficult and sensitive subject.

I especially want to praise God for my friends, Richard and Susannah, for agreeing to be part of this book and for courageously retelling their story, even when it brought so many fresh tears that it had to be done in stages. The Strawsons are an amazing family in the church we went to before our move to Manchester. They are full of life, hope and the desire to live for God and bless others. Susannah is a faith-filled warrior who challenges me about how much a mum of four can achieve and Richard is a gentle and godly example of fatherhood and service.

One day Susannah told me the wonderful news that they were pregnant again. Number Three. She was so excited and expectant. I remember her reading books about supernatural childbirth and telling me what she was learning. Daniel was born safe and well and I had a lovely cuddle with him when I visited to take round some food. Our small church celebrated the new arrival and I was part of the team that led worship at baby Daniel's dedication. At first Daniel was a normal, healthy child, as far as we could all tell. He had a gorgeously settled personality and would happily snuggle into whoever was holding him. But all too soon things started changing for him. The first indicators that something was wrong were on holiday in August at Bridport in Dorset. He was noticeably not himself and not smiling generally. The family began to see a pattern developing of him being sick with regularity and not wanting food. Sometimes he was pulling his head to one side and occasionally his mouth would form a strange shape and he would have what Susannah could only describe at the time as an 'Elvis lip'.

Susannah rang us with a very different tone in her voice to usual: 'Ems, I am so worried about Daniel. He has been behaving so strangely, and is just not himself.' I tried to reassure her and suggest simple things that might be wrong.

Initially Susannah was more concerned than Richard. She would point things out to him that seemed odd, but as they talked about it, they could always find another reasonable explanation. Perhaps she was just being over-cautious? The 'symptoms' could have pointed to so many other plausible 'baby' things: weaning, teething, and possibly even ear infections. At one stage they thought he might have developed a food allergy or some kind of intolerance. She confided in friends who said it could just be Daniel's little quirky ways. But the symptoms continued and they both became less convinced by their own answers.

Susannah became increasingly anxious and uncharacteristically protective about Daniel. It was the loss of weight that caused her the most concern, which was picked up by the regular visits to the baby clinic. They became more worried too when his cry became 'pathetic' – a word they hate to use, but it summed up the sad little noises he was making. He seemed to need more support doing simple things like sitting up as well. There were too many things going on now. It was time to go to the doctor.

The following Sunday they came up to the front and the whole church surrounded them with prayer, crying out to God for a straightforward diagnosis, for peace and for his healing. I looked at Susannah and Richard holding hands and hugging Daniel and their two other children, Thomas and Hannah. Susannah was gently rocking Daniel backwards and forwards like all mothers instinctively do when they want to lull their baby off to sleep.

They looked so sad and yet so strong.

Those two things were to sum them up in the months that followed.

DIFFICULT NEWS

Following frequent visits to the GP, a referral was made for Daniel to the Open Clinic at Pembury Hospital in Kent. All his tests came back negative, including an EEG to measure brain activity.

But on Friday 28 September he had his last test, an MRI scan. Daniel was sedated before being taken to the scanner and during the scan he needed extra oxygen to keep his condition stable. The result of the MRI was shocking. Their worst fears were realised.

Daniel was found to have a brain stem tumour.

That Friday evening, Richard travelled with Daniel to King's College Hospital by ambulance where they were hoping to remove the tumour in surgery. Daniel was then eight months old.

I can remember this day well. I sobbed on Jon's shoulder in my kitchen. There was a huge outpouring of love and grief from the church family. None of us could believe that such a perfect little baby could have cancer. It just didn't seem real.

But there was hope! Everyone was suddenly praying for Daniel's health and healing. There was a huge surge of faith and prayer in the church.

'What are you praying for?' people would ask me. 'For healing, for God's will, for strength to bear whatever comes...' I said. I didn't dare to say 'I don't know.' But sometimes, I think that was more like the truth.

Even on the very worst days, Richard and Susannah found themselves being able to trust God, lifting the situation to him, whatever the outcome. They were truly inspiring to be around. There was no 'Why us?' or 'How could God do this to our precious baby?' from their lips. They had an almost child-like dependence on God. They didn't hide their fears, but they didn't live by them either. There was continued prayer for Daniel and support and encouragement from friends and family alike.

Not knowing how things would turn out was scary. But having their Christian friends and family constantly administering everything they

WHISPER
A
DOXOLOGY
IN
THE
DARK

BRENNAN MANNING

needed from meals to hugs, made a huge difference. When we realised they were going to need to be near Daniel at King's, we made contact with the Salvation Army there who I had worked for a year or two earlier. They were incredibly kind and allowed the family to stay at their William Booth training centre for two and a half weeks. When the residents at the college needed the room back, the hospital told them of a vacancy at the Ronald McDonald house nearer the hospital. So they were even nearer to Daniel and were given an en suite room, a kitchen to make their own meals, space for Thomas and Hannah to 'sleep over' and washing facilities – in their hour of need, God had upgraded them!

Following surgery and the biopsy, Richard and Susannah were given yet more devastating news; the tumour was discovered to be a very rare and aggressive type of cancer for which there was no treatment in a child so young. (The tumour is called an AT/RT – an atypical teratoid rhabdoid tumour.)

After the full diagnosis and prognosis was given, Richard remembers a surreal moment, coming out of the hospital, getting some money out of the cash machine and having a sandwich at a local coffee shop. There was normal life going on all around them but they had just been told such overwhelming news. Nothing could be done for their little baby boy. He was going to die.

They have since remembered that there was a pub opposite the coffee shop they were in that was called The Perseverance. They both looked at the pub, looked at each other and began to well up – they both felt as if God was saying 'persevere.'

The tumour was stuck to Daniel's brain stem and so removal was very dangerous, a small amount of membrane had to be left. The tumour was therefore very likely to regrow aggressively and it was suggested that Daniel would live for only around three months. There was at the time no truly detailed information about this type of tumour.

Daniel had the operation to remove as much of the tumour as possible. The surgery went well and he was much better for a few weeks. At King's, the family met lots of others whose situations seemed far worse on the surface than Daniel's. On the ward there were other 'head injury' cases and Daniel often looked like the most well child there. He had good colour, a gorgeous smile and bright, blue eyes. There was no swelling to his face. His problems were all hidden. He remained beautiful throughout his illness. He was a happy baby again after the initial recovery of the operation. The bulk of the tumour had been taken away and so he was 'better' than he had been. Other children looked very poorly although they had more common conditions that were treatable. I was quite shocked when I went to visit him the day after his operation. I expected him to look awful. Of course he had his tubes in and was surrounded by the many beeping machines of intensive care. But he did not look that ill.

I began to wonder if he would get better. Each time I prayed, I had peace about him being in God's arms. I did not know the outcome. I remember singing Matt Redman's 'The Father's Song' over him in his cot one day in his ward.

'I have heard so many songs
Listened to a thousand tongues
But there is one that sounds above them all:
The Father's song
The Father's love
You sung it over me and for eternity
It's written on my heart.'[2]

It made me cry. It made Susannah cry. But it did not make Daniel cry. He gurgled away peacefully.

One day I painted Daniel a simple picture of a happy lion. I gave it to the family soon after he was admitted to Lion Ward at King's College Hospital. On the original drawing I wrote the following prayer:

'Dear Jesus, please be with Daniel just like you were with Daniel in the Lion's Den. Please use everything that happens to him to show others something beautiful about you. Amen.'

Richard and Susannah attached the picture to his cot and it became a symbol for them and for us all. They even had a special surgeon's head mask made with the Lion on it for Dr Chris Chandler, the surgeon who performed Daniel's operation.

The family met all sorts of people in that children's ward. Sometimes they were able to share very deeply and honestly with these vulnerable families and Richard experienced a new boldness and a natural ability to talk about his faith. It was hard for them in some ways that Daniel's condition was so extremely rare, as there was no one on the ward 'like them,' going through what they were facing.

Having said that, both had opportunities to share and to pray with one particular couple whose daughter died whilst they were there. Some of the things the mother shared with them felt like a preparation for them for the days ahead. They came across some inspirational parents who shared their faith and lived hopeful lives, but sadly, and understandably, there were also families who were really struggling with bitterness and anger and who felt unable to move past those emotions.

During this time they received many verses of hope from Christian friends and felt very sustained. Susannah marked them in her Bible to help her to pray and focus. The church organised prayer sessions and gave the family a large board on which verses, prayers, dreams, pictures and words of encouragement were written, including some from the children. A regular email update was sent out by Susannah's brother to a large number of people across the world and this became a very useful tool for them to communicate their prayer needs. Susannah used texting as her main method of communication with her closest friends and received much-needed encouragement from the replies.

But despite all the prayer for healing and wholeness this side of heaven, Daniel's condition got progressively worse.

The whole family had a lot of juggling to do. Richard and Susannah tried to be with their other children as much as possible. Life was disjointed and disruptive and Daniel's needs were so pressing. They aimed to be as open as possible with Thomas and Hannah – trying to allow them to talk and share all their feelings openly. They never led them to believe that Daniel would get better, or that he would die. They told them that he was very poorly and they would be praying for him to get better, but that they didn't know what Jesus' plan for Daniel was, only that he would look after him.

Trying to split their time with all three children was tough, travelling to and from London. Richard went back and forth to Kent to work most days during the five weeks they were at King's. The children missed their parents so much, but they were happier in their own home with their grandparents looking after them. Susannah would come home once a week for a big cuddle session and some 'normality'. During those times she would try and reassure the others in the family about how Daniel was, giving them thoughts for their own prayers.

When Daniel was back at Pembury and able to join the family at home for three weeks they built some great memories. This was an especially precious but exhausting time for Richard and Susannah, having to manage Daniel's care, be mindful of one another and care for the needs of their other children, too. But they coped so well. One day Susannah brought Daniel over to visit my family at home. I felt guilty as my three little healthy boys tore around the playroom as Daniel sat lolloped against Susannah with a tube taped to his tiny face. He was such a brave little soul. And his Mummy even more so.

During those precious weeks as home, Thomas and Hannah were able to be more involved in Daniel's day-to-day care and in his nasogastric feeds which gave them real bonding time together. Daniel would join them at the meal table and was able to have baths with them again. These were special and unforgettable days for the family.

Sadly they were not to last. After a weekend where he had not seemed his usual cheerful self, Daniel was suddenly very sick following a feed. He stopped breathing and his heart stopped beating.

At that exact time, I was giving my son, Sam, a snack at the kitchen table. He suddenly stopped eating and said, 'Mummy, why is baby Daniel in the sky?'

I spat my tea out in shock.

'What do you mean, darling?' I asked, wiping my mouth and wondering what on earth my three year old was talking about.

'Baby Daniel is in the sky,' he repeated, as if it was truly obvious.

Sam had sometimes had pictures given to him by God as a small child and I learnt to take notice of them. I wondered if he had pictured Daniel dying and going to be with Jesus, and called Susannah's mobile. I couldn't get through and wondered if all was well.

But God clearly decided that he did not want to call Daniel home quite yet. Through the prompt actions of Susannah with her friends Maxine and Jane, Daniel was speedily resuscitated and given oxygen to stabilise him. The Kent Air Ambulance and a ground crew were at the scene in minutes and took over to provide all the critical care Daniel needed. Richard rushed home from work and was able to go with Daniel to Maidstone Hospital by helicopter. Sam had seen Daniel in the sky after all.

Daniel was re-admitted to King's for those last two weeks and things began to change very fast. Every day seemed to bring new concerns and worries. The children could see the deterioration in their little brother and the worry in their parent's faces. Richard and Susannah didn't insist that they all visited Daniel everyday – it was their choice. It was the Christmas holidays and so, practically, they felt it would be better to be at home with Thomas and Hannah. They would travel up to spend time with Daniel, but it was so hard leaving him behind each time, they just wanted to be altogether.

> 'To be grateful for an unanswered prayer, to give thanks in a state of interior desolation, to trust in the love of God in the face of the marvels, cruel circumstances, obscenities, and commonplaces of life is to whisper a doxology in the dark.'
>
> Brennan Manning[3]

DETERIORATION

It became more difficult to visit as they sensed he was slipping away. Deep-seated fears began to creep in, and in some ways they felt scared to go in and see him. Whilst they were visiting Daniel one day there was a death in another part of the ward. A corner of the very small room was curtained off making the atmosphere so very different that day.

The family hadn't been given any 'timings' from the hospital, only that they don't like to keep children on the ventilator for too long and two weeks was a guide. On the evening of Sunday December 30, as Richard and Susannah walked out of the hospital, Richard said, 'I don't think he is going to come out of PICU.'

When they got home, they spent time praying and said the Lord's Prayer together out loud. Susannah remembers getting on her knees and saying, 'God, I can't cope if you don't heal him!' Then she added, 'Please heal him, or please look after him for me.'

Daniel was deteriorating and they were unable to remove him from the dependency of the ventilator. He began to have 'blue' episodes, where he needed even more help.

Richard told me later, 'The day after, Susannah was at the hospital, I was at work and she called to say that Daniel was not going to make it through the day . We talked and decided that I would collect Thomas and Hannah from her parents and travel to King's together to say goodbye. I remember driving to Susannah's mum's, trying to prepare myself for what I would say to the children.'

'I came to a realisation that nothing could prepare me for what I would say and gave up even trying to rehearse anything. The children were their normal happy selves when I arrived. Margaret gathered them around when I arrived and I just said something like that it was time for Daniel to go to heaven. He was not going to have any more pain. We cried and hugged each other – such emotions!'

> 'In all their distress he too was distressed, and the angel of his presence saved them. In his love and mercy he redeemed them; he lifted them up and carried them all the days of old.'
>
> Isaiah 63:9[4]

Daniel was being called home, to the World's Best Dad and to an eternal home with no pain. Daniel went to be with his Heavenly Father on New Year's Eve, 2007 at 5pm, aged 11 months.

Immediately after his death, Susannah told me she felt as if someone had ripped her heart out. It was like there was a physical hole there, often accompanied by feelings of deep sickness. It was an indescribable weight of such magnitude she found it hard to talk about. She could not believe that the son who had grown and lived inside her, that she had given birth to, was no longer physically there. She just wanted him back so badly. She sat, comforting herself with his teddy which still had Daniel's smell on it.

The children were devastated. Thomas felt sad, upset and had times of feeling very hurt that Daniel had died. Hannah desperately missed her little brother.

Richard was deeply upset and had great fears for the future. How would people in the family, especially Susannah, handle this? How would they all cope with the loss and the change? There was such an emptiness without Daniel. Something, someone was constantly missing. The whole pattern of their lives changed. No more visits to hospital. No more medication. No more little Daniel.

> 'Grief puts us squarely in the middle of a fire. It burns away everything that is not essential to our lives'
> Alana Sheeren[5]

Daniel's funeral was a heartrendingly moving service. His 'treasure box', as the family described his coffin, was decorated with the Lion picture. It was so beautiful and made leading worship a very emotional affair indeed.

Later, they held a much bigger service in a local town and so many people came to celebrate Daniel's life. The family gave everyone a candle with Daniel's lion on it and also some pictures of him. Many of Richard and Susannah's friends rallied round to help them and stand with them.

After the funeral and thanksgiving service, life felt very strange for the family for a long time. Susannah remembers being at home on her own, just sitting and sighing and crying. It felt so hard and so odd not to be pushing the pushchair up the road to the school. It was such a lonely time in those first few weeks and months. She didn't really want to be comforted either, she just needed to be on her own. She would come home from the school run and just sit and look at pictures of Daniel by herself, trying her best to come to terms with her loss. She would look through his clothes and his toys, imagining him, crying and smelling things which still smelt of him.

In those early days of grief, Susannah had a close network of family and friends to support her. She would be escorted to school, so she never had to be on her own in the playground. It was like a buffer, that people had to get through to speak to her. She needed that protection. People would come up to her and say, 'I don't know what to say!' But she didn't either. Nothing made much difference. A hug was usually the best way of communicating what could not be said.

'There is, I am convinced, no picture that conveys in all its dreadfulness, a vision of sorrow, despairing, remediless, supreme. If I could paint such a picture, the canvas would show only a woman looking down at her empty arms.'

Charlotte Bronte[6]

THE JOURNEY OF GRIEF

Richard and Susannah learnt very quickly not to be offended by what was said or written in letters, emails and cards. Many people simply didn't know how to respond and sometimes said things that they found inappropriate, insensitive and hard to hear and deal with. Both she and Richard had times when they used to wonder whether they could have done anything more for Daniel to prevent his condition. Did they get him to the doctor in time? Could his problems have been picked up at an earlier stage? Did they miss any of his symptoms? Richard remembers needing to reject a sense of irrational and unfounded guilt that came to him a few times for not being with Daniel more when he was alive. They still very occasionally have difficult thoughts like these, but when they talk together about it they feel a sense of comfort that everything that happened was for a reason. Looking back they can now see God's perfect timing in Daniel's life.

The family tried to grieve together as much as possible, sometimes watching home videos of them all with Daniel on holiday. Thomas and Hannah had counselling with a Christian counsellor, something Richard and Susannah both felt was really important to help to prevent any issues later in life. The family also had the amazing help of a Play Specialist from Rainbow Trust. He came and supported them whilst Daniel was poorly, but continued to visit after Daniel died to make memory boxes with Thomas and Hannah. The children have great memories of him. He was someone who was really impacted by Daniel's life. Also, Demelza Bereaved Families, and Siblings Group was a great lifeline. Thomas and Hannah are still invited on various events and the family have been involved in a new 'Garden of Tranquillity' to remember all the children who have died. At times the children would go to bed and start talking about Daniel and how they missed him, and then the whole family would all get upset. From time-to-time they still wander downstairs and plonk themselves on the settee and say they are 'sad about Daniel'. They have a cuddle, a pray and some tears (then get sent back to bed!) Richard and Susannah didn't feel that they needed any specific counselling. They both have a supportive and very caring church family to keep an eye on them, and of course their own family. The family found it a great comfort to hear people say how they missed Daniel like he was their own.

Thomas wrote on Friday, January 28, 2011:

'Today it is Daniel's Day (His birthday)(He's 4). After school we went bowling & Mummy won! Back at home we lit 4 star sparklers. 4 for how old he would have been if he was still with us. We sang Happy Birthday and may God bless you.

And may God bless you.
And love you and Keep you.
Happy Birthday to you!!!!'

WHAT NOW?

Daniel's legacy is a rich one. His short life has made a huge difference to many people. Knowing him for those short months changed the Strawson's lives and their focus forever. Rather than being a family bound up in trauma or self pity they have channelled their emotions into caring for others. Richard now works as a phone-line volunteer for the Great Ormond Street Hospital Child Death Helpline which he finds very valuable and helpful for himself as well as others. The family are also working on starting some kind of local hub for parents and families in similar situations.

Susannah told me, 'Daniel touched so many other people's lives not just ours. Knowing him has given me a big appetite for all the things of Heaven and when I hear of another person being promoted there I always think of Daniel and how he might be making them feel welcome. The death of a child is something you never expect to have to cope with. But we have come out "the other side" as a stronger family who still have faith! It has changed us, too. We feel that we have more empathy for those with cancer, and with bereaved parents and families of children. Having the privilege and honour of caring for Daniel has made us appreciate and value each other more. His life has left us with a passion to one day open a pre-school nursery for children with life-limiting and terminal illnesses – Daniel's Dandelion House! I have begun writing a book called *Keep Praying, Keep Praising* which is all about Daniel and our family's "journey"' I hope one day to have it published – but we will see!'

For the whole family, life has changed a great deal. Richard and Susannah have gone on to have two more little girls, Lydia and Faith. Thomas sometimes finds it hard that he is not able to support his little brother, but he is able to thank God that Daniel is safe in heaven. He remembers Daniel in his prayers.

For Daniel's sister Hannah, the most difficult thing was having to face the fact that Daniel had gone. She wrote this acrostic poem in memory of him when she was 6 years old.

D aniel
A ngel
N ever without Jesus
I ternal brother and sister
E ver near
L ive for ever

You can find out more information about Daniel on the website dedicated to him: www.danielstrawson.org.uk

SHARING OUR STORY

Earlier today I was chatting to a lady I don't know very well in a queue. She asked me what I do and so I shared a little about this book I am writing. She listened hard before telling me the sad story of her close friend whose baby girl died in late pregnancy. She shared how this person feels she has not just lost her baby, but lost herself, too. She asked whether I could recommend anything that would help her. Suddenly the queue parted as someone came through with a buggy and we were separated. I couldn't find her afterwards.

It made me realise again how precious the opportunities are to share in people's grief. Those of us who believe in the God of the Bible know something to bring hope. More than this, we know SOMEONE who has conquered death.

The best thing I could offer this lady wouldn't be counselling or CBT or acupuncture or dance classes... but the Holy Trinity. Three persons in one, all willing us on, comforting us in our times of need, strengthening us in difficulty and translating our groans into prayers. I pray I meet her again soon.

I came across this song by Bob Dylan recently and found the words a real comfort:

'When you're sad and when you're lonely
And you haven't got a friend
Just remember that death is not the end

And all that you held sacred
Falls down and does not mend
Just remember that death is not the end

Not the end, not the end
Just remember that death is not the end

When you're standin' on the crossroads
That you cannot comprehend
Just remember that death is not the end

And all your dreams have vanished
And you don't know what's up the bend
Just remember that death is not the end

Not the end, not the end
Just remember that death is not the end

When the storm clouds gather round you
And heavy rains descend
Oh, the tree of life is growing

Where the spirit never dies
And the bright light of salvation shines
In dark and empty skies

Not the end, not the end

Just remember that death is not the end.'[7]

HE MAKES ME LIE DOWN

LOSING YOUR HEALTH

'The Lord is my shepherd, I lack nothing.
He makes me lie down in green pastures, he leads me
beside quiet waters, he refreshes my soul.
He guides me along the right paths for his name's sake.
Even though I walk through the darkest valley, I will
fear no evil, for you are with me; your rod and your
staff, they comfort me.'

Psalm 23:1–4[1]

THE THUNDERCLAP

Saturday May 11, 2013 started like most others for Mike. A fit man who enjoys training and exercise, he got up as usual and prepared himself for his normal 5k park run. He was hoping to beat his personal best.

Together with a friend and around a hundred or so other runners, he set off from the start line. But not long into the race a terrible shooting pain attacked Mike in the back of his head and neck. This wasn't a normal headache. It was as though he had been hit with a baseball bat.

He thought it may just be a severe muscle spasm at first and tried to continue running. But after a few more steps he simply couldn't keep moving. He was overcome with nausea and dizziness, so he wandered slowly back to the finishing line to wait for his friend who was still running. His initial thought was that he had a meningitis type condition. The headache was more severe than anything he had ever experienced.

After finding his friend, Mike weakly began to drive them both home. His friend asked on a number of occasions if he could drive, but as Mike struggles with motion sickness as a passenger, he decided to carry on driving himself. At one stage, he had to stop and pull over. He stood against a wall trying to breathe deeply and battle the desire to vomit, or faint, or both.

He gently got back into the car and caught sight of himself in the rear view mirror. His face was a washed-out-grey. He looked as awful as he felt. He thought he would feel better after a lie down. After what seemed like the longest drive, he eventually got home and took himself to bed. The paracetamol he took didn't touch the awful thumping pain in his head. In fact it seemed to be getting worse.

He reached out for his phone and slowly texted his wife, Helen, who was downstairs. All he could manage was: 'Can you come to bedroom. I'm ill.'

Helen came up immediately. She was alarmed at Mike's colour and his condition. They decided he had to see a doctor. Somehow he got downstairs and into the car. The agony of his headache was intense. He had to hold his head and the back of his neck as the pressure he was feeling was overwhelmingly painful.

SERIOUS NEWS

The nurse who saw him allowed him to see a doctor very quickly and he was immediately referred to Stepping Hill hospital. At the hospital he waited in a queue for about an hour with his head feeling like it was about to explode. Helen was worried and texted a few key friends to ask them to pray.

Even before Mike knew he was being prayed for, he experienced a sudden lessening of his symptoms. He described it as almost like a switch was being turned on. When Mike realised that Helen had texted people for prayer he was initially not very pleased. He is not the kind of man who wants to be the centre of attention and does not like a big fuss made about anything if he can help it. But even he had to acknowledge that the prayers of those Helen had contacted were beginning to make a difference.

When he finally saw a doctor, Mike's symptoms had begun to ease slightly, so he hoped that he would be allowed to go home. But he was then given a CT scan as part of the tests to check for any abnormalities in his body. Very soon after the scan had finished, a doctor rushed into the room.

'Lie down! Lie down!' he said imperatively. 'You have had a brain haemorrhage. I have called an ambulance to transfer you to Hope Hospital in Salford which has a specialist neurological unit.'

This was hard to take in.

'It can't be good if one hospital is rushing you to another one,' Mike thought to himself. 'That is never good.'

Mike needed to go to the loo.

'No! You can't get up. You must stay lying down,' explained the doctor. 'Don't move!'

Mike and Helen were shell-shocked. What was happening? Only a few hours ago everything was normal and now... now they were facing a very dangerous and life-threatening situation.

Helen sent this simple but scary text message: 'Mike has had a bleed. He's being transferred to Hope Hospital by ambulance. I'll keep you posted.'

Many more people heard the news and started praying in earnest for Mike and he and Helen both began to be even more aware of their prayers.

WORRIES AND WIKIPEDIA

Mike was given paracetemol and a drug called Nimodipine which is prescribed to prevent major complications following what doctors termed a 'subarachnoid haemorrhage.' These two words were ones Mike had never had to associate with himself before. He wasn't even sure what 'subarachnoid' meant. So he did what anyone would do with access to a smartphone: he looked it up on Wikipedia. He was horrified by what he read. He didn't dare share it with Helen.

> 'SAH is a form of stroke and comprises 1–7% of all strokes. It is a medical emergency and can lead to death or severe disability— even when recognised and treated at an early stage. Up to half of all cases of SAH are fatal and 10–15% of casualties die before reaching a hospital, and those who survive often have neurological or cognitive impairment.'[2]

Mike felt even more sick.

Helen was feeling a combination of numbness and disbelief. She deliberately did not investigate the prognosis online as she didn't want her faith to be limited by what she read.

Being online via a smartphone from a hospital bed may not have been helpful from a self-diagnosis perspective, but it was wonderful to receive texts, emails and social media messages from friends and family. As soon as he arrived in the hospital Mike started to see all the texts and emails from friends saying there were praying. Each message and prayer was another source of hope that God was in this situation with him and Helen.

One particularly precious email was sent to Mike by the friend who was with him during the original park run.

> 'Have you not known? Have you not heard? The LORD is the everlasting God, the Creator of the ends of the earth. He does not faint or grow weary; his understanding is unsearchable. He gives power to the faint, and to him who has no might he increases strength. Even (Mike) shall faint and be weary, and shall fall exhausted; but when (Mike) waits for the Lord He shall renew your strength; you shall mount up with wings like eagles; you shall run and not be weary; you shall walk and not faint.' (Based on the words of Isaiah 40:28-31)

My own message to Mike included these words:

> 'I am utterly crying out to God for you as I write this and asking for His continued protection and mercy on your life and well being.

> I pray that even though you are faced with so many questions, uncertainties and unknowns right now that you can know the truth of the phrase 'It is well with my soul!' because of the knowledge that you are being carried and upheld by heavenly angels. (He WILL command His angels to guard you and watch over you in ALL your ways)'

'God may be refining you and teaching you many things but His desire is that you come out with more GOLD in you than before the trial. I pray GOLD into each conversation, thought and prayer you share with others and with Him.'

'Praying for your healing and your inner man to know the deep and crazy peace of God that makes no sense. Praying against worry, fear and doubt. Praying for faith to rise in you and tears to be few.'

'We will be remembering you every hour of tomorrow by setting an alarm on our phones.'

'God does not need such an alarm does He?! He is interceding for you right now!'

> 'Miracles are not contrary to nature, but only contrary to what we know about nature.'
>
> St Augustine[3]

FACING THE FEARS

Meanwhile the drug Mike had been given was making his headache worse. It was forcing open the arteries and making him feel as though someone was banging his temples with a mallet with every heartbeat.

Every hour he was being observed and similar questions were being asked to check his cognitive function.

What's your name?
What year is it?
Who is the Prime Minister?
Do you know where you are?
What day is it?

His initial interactions with the doctors at Hope Hospital were deeply upsetting. Armed with the knowledge that Wikipedia had afforded him, he was also told that he would very likely now suffer some kind of stroke.

This was a very low moment for him. He struggled to come to terms with what his life would be like now.

Helen sent this text:

> 'Please pray! Doctors telling him his condition could deteriorate over next few weeks. He is understandably scared and upset. We are hanging on by our fingertips here! Also that it could take a year to recover. Could be life changing. Scan today. Op tomorrow. We're upset!'

I received this message and shouted the word 'No!' into my phone. I prayed, like many others that day, for an opposite diagnosis for Mike.

A number of people in the church felt it was right to start a Daniel Fast as we prayed for him. One lady (not someone who knows the family that well) told me that she simply couldn't stop crying. For around three days she cried almost hourly.

God was stirring up His people.

Another text came in from Helen:

> 'I have just left him, alert and comfortable, after visiting hour there. He had a CT scan this afternoon and tomorrow the consultants will decide the best treatment for him. This may well be an operation to repair the damage. Christians are not immune to life's troubles. The difference perhaps lies in the hope and trust we have in Jesus that we have as we respond to them. Thanks for praying for him everyone. He has really appreciated all your texts but has a headache so isn't replying but is trying to rest for now. In fact he's not allowed to sit up!'

Even though Mike wasn't experiencing any stroke-like symptoms, he was told these could easily happen over the following few days and weeks. He kept hoping he was over the worst, but medics were warning him that this could be just the beginning of some very life-changing months ahead.

PEACE IN THE STORM

Mike describes himself as someone who tends to panic and worry in times of crisis. For him, going to the dentist is bad enough. But throughout what should have been an overwhelmingly terrifying situation, he felt strangely peaceful and calm. Having his brain examined live and being told he would experience sensations behind his eye or near his tongue should have been awful for him. But all the way through the dreadful explorations and tests, he felt calm and at peace.

He knew that HAD to be the power and presence of God at work. Although he was finding it hard to pray because of the pain he was in, he felt others were somehow praying his prayers for him.

> 'There I was, still in my running gear, in my ward, surrounded by five other men who were mostly on feeding tubes and unable to speak. The prospect of my condition worsening to the point where I would be in a similar position was frightening. My greatest fear was that I would be severely handicapped at the end of my treatment. In terms of handling the fear, I took each hour at a time. There was nothing I could do about the situation – I just had to put my faith in God.'

MONDAY MIRACLE

On the Monday, Mike had an angiogram to try to locate the source of the bleeding. The church was together praying that evening when the consultant came to tell him that they could not locate the source of the bleed but it had 'healed itself'. He told Mike that his outlook was good and there would no need for any further treatment. Mike and Helen were able to communicate this information to the church prayer meeting via text.

Those of us at the prayer meeting clapped and cheered God hard with tears of gratefulness in our eyes and thankfulness in our hearts. Mike had been miraculously healed! Doctors told him he needed no other treatment.

After he was allowed home, five days after the bleed, he needed some time to recover. His back was sore and stiff and he walked like a tin soldier. He still had a fairly bad residual headache, but nothing like what he had suffered before. The blood that had been loose in his brain was dispersing down and around his body and this meant he felt pretty groggy, but he knew he was getting better. The whole church was bearing Mike up in prayer and he knew it. He and Helen sent the following email to church members just five days after his brain bleed:

'As you may be aware Mike suffered a brain haemorrhage whilst on a 5km run last Saturday morning. He spent Saturday to Wednesday in Salford Royal Hospital Neurological Unit but is now back at home after what we believe is a 'miraculous' recovery.'

'Throughout all of the investigations and treatments of the last few days, we have known God's presence and peace, plus a humbling level of love and support from the church. Mike's initial symptoms of intense headache began to ease, only when church friends began to pray. When the consultant warned of potential long term brain damage, encouraging words and prayers poured in. As doctors pushed probes around the inside of Mike's brain (whilst he was awake!) looking for the bleed, he was able to spiritually hold on to Jesus as friends prayed him through. When news from the consultant confirmed that the source of the bleed had 'healed itself', we were able to text the amazing news to church friends as they prayed together at the church centre.

We are now more convinced than ever of these truths:

1. God is with us in EVERY circumstance and is using each one for HIS glory.
2. Prayer WORKS. We need to pray for one another more and more.
3. Ivy Manchester and its church family are ONE IN A MILLION.

Thank you from the bottom of our hearts for all your support and prayers. As Anthony often says 'WE LOVE OUR CHURCH'.

'Miracles are a retelling in small letters of the very same story which is written across the whole world in letters too large for some of us to see.'

C.S. Lewis[4]

Mike and Helen described the support from their church family as absolutely amazing. They have been completely stunned by how loving and supportive people have been. This is one of the aspects of the incident they will never forget. Mike and Helen used to dream about moving to the coast or the countryside or emigrating, but there is no way they would want to leave the group of people God has placed them in now.

I asked Mike why he thinks God healed him so miraculously.

'God has not finished with me yet! I guess there was something more that God still wants me to do for him! If He can get me through what I have been through, He can help us pray with other people in difficult circumstances. He can help in any situation we are up against. He will answer.'

Mike now understands more fully that Christians like him aren't exempt from challenges in life. He received a few words about 'being refined by fire' so he is fascinated to see how life develops and what else God teaches him.

Mike smiled shyly before continuing.

'God has a wonderful plan for each of our lives. For some people that plan is for them to continue in this life. I believe that God has things left for me to accomplish here on earth and last month wasn't my time to die. There are many things I want to see completed during my lifetime, such as my children growing up and our church flourishing. I think God has those dreams for me too.'

I suppose my prayers were asking God to allow me to carry on 'my race' to reach my own personal finish line. My key challenge in the next few weeks is a return to work. I need to have a sharp memory and be able to work quickly and handle pressure. Time will tell whether I will be able to continue in the same work role or start a new chapter in my life.'

'Certainly, other people can pray for you, they can believe for you, they can quote the scripture to you, but you must exercise faith for yourself. If you are always depending on somebody else to keep you happy, somebody else to encourage you or to get you out of trouble, you will live in perpetual weakness and disappointment. You must make a decision that you are going to be a believer. Take charge of your life and decide, 'No matter what comes against me, I believe in God. I'm going to have a positive outlook for my life! Other people's faith can indeed bolster yours. But your own faith will bring you a miracle much faster than anybody else's. What you believe has a much greater impact on your life than what anybody else believes.'

Joel Osteen[5]

At the time of writing, Mike is one month on from the incident and his recovery has been good. He is trying to put the whole experience behind him. Mike is praying that there will be no lasting damage to his cognitive ability. He is still a bit dizzy when being driven in a car. Remembering names seems to be even harder than usual at the moment, but far less than he was told to expect. All things considered, he is doing amazingly well.

The nurses described how some people become fearful of the situation which they believed 'caused' their haemorrhage. Mike has not tried running again, and doesn't think he will try to run 5k or 10k at his fastest pace again in the future. But outside of this specific area, he has been blessed not to have any feelings of panic and fear. In fact, he is currently thinking about taking up cycling!

LONG-SUFFERING GOD

Why did Mike go through this situation?

Why does God allow us to journey through seasons like this?

Why do people have to face such hard things?

These are not easy questions and whole books have been written on the subject.

I don't pretend to know and I don't want to give any glib answers here. There is nothing worse than someone spouting unhelpful, vending-machine theology at you when you are going through trauma or pain. But I do what to share with you what I am learning about God's designs for me.

Firstly I have examined God's character more fully in the last few months and found out that He understands me more than I ever knew before.

The God of the Bible, my God and yours, possesses infinite wisdom (Psalm 147:5) and perfect character. I cannot fault Him, although I may not understand him. In order to grow in Christian maturity and be like him, we are to develop that same wonderful character (Matthew 5:48.) We might have some ideas and suggestions about how to go about that (!), but the best designer – the author and perfecter of our faith – has it well covered (Hebrews 12:2). He knows what we need in order to develop enough spiritual backbone to ensure we won't crumble when tough times come.

It was only very recently in my Bible study that I realised that God suffers too.

Read with me in the New King James version, 'But the fruit of the [Holy] Spirit is love, joy, peace, longsuffering, gentleness, goodness, faith, meekness, temperance...' (Galatians 5:22–23)[6]

In these verses God describes the character and nature of his Spirit as 'longsuffering.' This rather took me by surprise.

'MIRACLES ARE
NOT CONTRARY
TO NATURE,
BUT ONLY CONTRARY
TO WHAT WE KNOW
ABOUT NATURE'

ST AUGUSTINE

How does God suffer? And why in a 'long' sense?

Genesis 6:6 speaks of how God was grieved in His heart at the paths mankind had chosen and who they had become. Numbers 14:18 (NKJV) says, 'The LORD is longsuffering and abundant in mercy.' But this verse does not reveal why it is necessary for God to suffer. He is God. Why would he allow himself to feel any kind of pain? Surely he could just flick a switch in his heart and turn off anything unpleasant, couldn't he?

I think the answer to this question reveals perhaps the most amazing truth I have learnt about God for some time. Namely this: God chooses to feel suffering because of his intimate and intentional love for me and for you.

If you are privileged enough to have children you will understand that how they feel affects you deeply. If they are ill, hurt or struggling it grieves you too. You suffer with them when they are bullied, or afflicted or rejected. You feel their pain. You grieve.

God is the ultimate parent. He is the best father there is. To cut himself off from feelings of suffering would separate him from us in a way he could not allow. When we disobey Him, directly hurting ourselves in the process, it hurts him too. When we mourn, he mourns. He feels pain. Not just our pain, but pain all of his own. He grieves. This was a revelation to me.

SUFFERING AS GOD'S TOOL

I believe that suffering of any kind is therefore not an accident. It is not because God has temporarily lost a battle with the enemy but because He has won every battle there is. Each time we experience some kind of struggle, suffering or pain, God gets to work. He fashions each experience with his own hands using it to teach, bless and open us up to him in a new way. His goal? For us to be like him. He is longsuffering and we are meant to be, too.

Ecclesiastes 7:14 says, 'When things are going well for you, be happy, and when trouble comes, just remember: God sends both happiness and trouble...'[7]

If God sends both happiness and trouble, there is a reason for that. The purpose of our lives is to become more like God, to develop more of his character with every passing day. Suffering and pain are tied into building this kind of character.

> 'Imitate God, therefore, in everything you do, because you are his dear children. Live a life filled with love, following the example of Christ.'
>
> Ephesians 5:1-2[8]

WHY CHRIST SUFFERED

Many books have been written on the subject of Jesus' suffering so I have deliberately not focused on this subject for any length here. But I do want to point out one or two passages that have really helped me understand more of God's plans for his Son and for us.

Hebrew 5:7–9 says:

> 'While Jesus was here on earth, he offered prayers and pleadings, with a loud cry and tears, to the one who could rescue him from death. And God heard his prayers because of his deep reverence for God. Even though Jesus was God's Son, *he learned obedience* from the things he suffered. In this way, God qualified him as a perfect High Priest, and he became the source of eternal salvation for all those who obey him.' (my emphasis)[9]

Jesus was without sin, but this passage shows us that he learnt something from his suffering. In some incredible way pain completed Jesus' earthly experience. That astounds me! God allowed him to suffer, to go through everything we go through, to make him whole. Being made of flesh, just like you and me, God allowed him to experience and learn human lessons that he would otherwise not have known.

Hebrews 2:10 says, 'God is the one for whom and through whom everything exists. Therefore, while God was bringing many sons and daughters to glory, it was the right time to bring Jesus, the source of their salvation, to the end of his work through suffering.'[10]

Jesus endured his pain for us in order to learn what God wanted him to learn; more than this, so that he could be made perfect. So why do we go through pain? Perhaps for the very same reason.

C.S. Lewis has an interesting take on this: 'But pain insists upon being attended to. God whispers in our pleasures, speaks in our conscience, but shouts in our pains; it is His megaphone to rouse a deaf world.'[11]

I am not saying that all hardship will make us more like Jesus.

As Oswald Chambers writes: 'We all know people who have been made much meaner and more irritable and more intolerable to live with by suffering: it is not right to say that all suffering perfects. It only perfects one type of person... the one who accepts the call of God in Christ Jesus.'[12]

WHY DO WE SUFFER?

As we read earlier, Mike's physical pain was of sufficient intensity to stop him in his tracks. It literally crippled him. When we suffer we immediately look for a cause of our pain. We want to know why.

Hebrews 5:9 gives us a further clue about our reasons for pain. 'And being made perfect, he became the author of eternal salvation unto all them that obey Him.'[13]

Jesus became qualified to 'become the author of eternal salvation' because he was willing to endure and learn from God's prescribed suffering process for all who are His sons—those who obey him.

That means that when we suffer, we qualify for something greater too. What is this?

Paul also wrote, 'Here is a trustworthy saying: If we died with him, we will also live with him; if we endure, we will also reign with him'[14]

I do not like pain and I don't want to suffer.

But I am starting to realise that there is deep value in my grief and how I have started to process it. If I am in submission to God, suffering in any way will make me more like Jesus. Suffering will allow me to 'reign' with him.

God allowed Jesus to suffer to make him whole. I believe that this is the purpose of grief and pain of all kinds.

Grief makes us whole because it makes us more like our incredible, longsuffering God.

LOST
CONNECTION
FEELING FAR FROM GOD

'Sometimes we wonder why these prayers are not being answered, and well-meaning people tell us deep things about prayer not being a slot machine, or about the transforming inner power of contemplative prayer, or about fasting, spiritual warfare and the importance of gratitude. We nod and say, "Aha, that's really helpful," but our prayer lives continue to be a staccato succession of yells and groans like a man falling down the stairs.'

Pete Grieg[1]

One of the most frightening things for a Christian is what happens if we suddenly begin to doubt God's reality, goodness, presence, or ability. Any one of those is a scary premise; fearing all of them is awful.

When a person who professes to be a Christian begins to struggle with knowing the identity and character of God or Christ, it can affect our own identity, too. We will start to wonder who we are and maybe even why we are alive at all.

Let me be honest with you and say that I have felt very disappointed by God this year. He didn't appear to me to be very majestic. There weren't many miracles, there wasn't much joy and he certainly didn't win any prizes from me for his clear and unequivocal direction. It seemed as though he was bored of me. Sometimes I even entertained the idea that he might be being cruel. I questioned his kindness and I critically examined his methods and his motives. My faith was intact. God was definitely there. But my trust was in tatters. He wasn't who I thought he was.

I was so disappointed. I felt so let down. Not just by God but by myself as well.

If there is one thing I can't stand it's Christians who whine on about how awful their lives are and don't realise how much God has given them. I despise people like that. But I was becoming 'Exhibit A'. I started to look down on myself. And when you start doing that for long, it can get a bit ugly. It's as pointless as moaning to your best friend that you are overweight as you stuff another doughnut into your mouth. There were so many things I didn't want to think and feel, but I just did. I know other people who have gone through similar sensations and emotions, battling with how they feel and desperately trying to be the opposite.

Over the past few months I have truly questioned my ability to trust God. I am not even sure why. I have gone through some pretty bad things in my life. I have suffered some fairly awful abuse, seen a friend drown, lost a close friendship, been accused of something shocking I did not do and lots of other nasty stuff in between. Grieving for my Mum and my Gran did not seem nearly as 'traumatic' as these in many ways. And yet it was life-shattering.

It caught me by surprise. It showed me that the level of my faith was not what I had imagined. I found myself wanting. I found myself laid low. I was hurt by my own lack of strength. I wanted to preach triumphantly to myself and quote endless scriptures in my dreams. But I could not. I was not able to find the depth of faith in myself that in my arrogance I had always thought was there.

LOSING TRUST

So what led me to feel such disappointment and despair? Why did I start to lose my trust in God?

I think part of it was the fact that he had allowed me to walk through more pain than I thought I could handle. I wasn't sure he was being kind and good anymore. I knew that he IS those things. But he seemed to be going 'off message' with me. It felt as though he was piling up more and more on my back. I felt like an overladen packhorse, with rickets! I was struggling under the weight of it all and forgot who was actually carrying me.

I think also that many of my prayers were not being answered the way I had hoped. I have seen people cast out demons, cut off soul ties, make declarations in the heavenly realms, utter long powerful scriptures, recite archaic hymns and scream the place down and miracles, genuine moves of God, have ensued. I tried it all. I fasted for months but God did not heal my Mum. I pleaded and prayed every day for her to be made well, but God chose to take her home instead. He did not let me be in charge once – and I was most displeased with him about it!

I think that much of what I was facing wasn't about losing my Mum but about losing my dreams and my hopes of what I would one day become. I didn't realise how much I had it all worked out in my head until it didn't happen exactly as I had hoped. I am somewhat embarrassed to admit it, but I was duped.

WHEN PROPHECY BECOMES A PROP

One of the hardest things I have had to cope with in recent years has been unhelpful or counterfeit prophecy. I am all for words that build us up and are encouraging but sometimes people take it too far and it becomes, 'What nice things can I say about this person that will make them skip down the hallway singing happy songs with abandon?' This has absolutely nothing to do with what God wants to speak over us at all and is as dangerous and misguided as a tarot card reading. A lot of prophecy in the Bible foretells difficult things, tough circumstances and unpleasant situations.

I am not saying that I would prefer people coming up to me and sharing their gloom-laden thoughts that my cat will get an unsightly disease or that my great aunt will have an accident on a banana boat and return to shore with a vicious head wound. But a bit of actual 'God's honest' truth would be good.

I realise now that I was angry with God for allowing me to think certain things that he had never told me in the first place. Other people had tickled my ears with things and I had assumed that they were of God. Sometimes lovely, godly people are hugely wide of the mark and at other times, they get the timing skewed or the wrong end of the stick. They may even interpret a genuine word from God the way they think it should be – when God actually meant something totally opposite to their understanding. It isn't their fault. We are all human. We all get things like that wrong. I know I have.

My problem was that I had begun to place too much importance on those words and not enough on trying to weigh them. (Have you noticed that we don't weigh words we like as much as the words we don't? We are happy to soak them up and preen ourselves a little. I shudder at the way I have done this.)

I have had well-meaning people tell me that I would be a famous singer, a TV presenter, a nurse, a speaker, a successful writer, a prophet... all sorts of crazy things. The trouble is that I started to believe in some of those ideas, rather than in the God who guides me.

Just because someone CAN do something, doesn't mean God wants them to do it full time, on a global scale, with a band of thousands cheering them on. It may be that he wants to hone in on something more subtle and unusual in their lives. A few of us are meant to live loudly and impressively where everyone notices everything we do. But most of us are called instead to a quieter, more ordinary, but just as sanctified, existence.

I think God has been trying to teach me this for years. The death of my Mum brought about a large reality check for me about what I was hoping my life would be like. It showed me that I was hoping for a 'grander' life than the one I had, and that I didn't actually trust God and his plans for me as much as I had believed. I felt cheated; cheated out of dreams I had and cheated that I had been given them in the first place. I was angry with the well-wishers, the faithful, lovely people who had spoken numbers and seasons and what they hoped for me by the age of 40. But none of it happened in the way they or I had thought.

I had not become a worship leader or a well-travelled, well-known speaker. I was not a writer of renown or any of the other things people had said over me. I was a Mum and a wife who occasionally went to Stockport. The only thing that I seemed to get better at over the few months after Mum died was baking and icing cakes. I am not knocking it, but it wasn't exactly life changing.

I looked at myself with disgust. Had I missed God's plan for me somehow? Had I taken the wrong path? What on earth was going on? At the same time as this, other people around me were receiving clear and direct words from God, their paths seemed to be aligning more towards their dreams and their lives seemed more fulfilled and purposeful than mine. I was genuinely happy for them and cheered them on, but about my own life... well, I was the Wikipedia definition of 'gutted.'

At this exact time I received an invitation to preach on a Sunday morning at church that had never happened before (or since). The theme of my talk was on trusting God in difficult times. Talk about irony! I nearly asked if I could bail out of it, but close friends advised me to carry on. I preached the sermon, primarily to myself, and struggled on.

I felt alone, but strangely, not abandoned. God was still there. He was silent, but not deaf. He could hear me loud and clear and I knew it. But I was so mad with him.

He was not interested in giving me an easy, safe, fun, meaningless life. He wanted to develop me, mould me, increase my capacity, channel me, challenge me and upset my equilibrium. He wanted to change my status and my horizons. He wanted to grow my faith.

The only thing was, I didn't want any of those things. I wanted him to comfort me and make it all go away.

> 'We work hard to disown the parts of our lives that were painful, difficult, or sad. But just as we can't rip chapters out of a book and expect the story to still make sense, so we cannot rip chapters out of our past and expect our lives to still make sense. Keep every chapter of your life intact, and keep on turning the pages.'
>
> Sandra Kring[2]

The verse in Proverbs 29:18 (KJV) 'Where there is no vision, the people perish...' came to me. I felt like I was perishing. Like cheap rubber.

I started to feel as though I was never going to recover, that I would always have this sense of gloom over me. (Which, of course, is exactly what the devil wants us all to feel isn't it? He loves to sow lies like this.)

DEPRESSION

A friend of mine (who wishes to remain anonymous) shared with me her own difficult experiences triggered by grief recently. I asked her if I could include her testimony here and she agreed.

She writes:

'I first became depressed around the age of 15. Many things had built up and led to the depression, including friendships, bullying and the deaths of people close to the family and family members. I didn't particularly realise that I was depressed until around a year or so later when life seemed much harder to bear. I felt completely isolated and alone. I needed some way of venting how I felt and I blamed myself for everything: it was my fault I had no friends, it was my fault nobody would listen to me etc.

At this point I began to self-harm. It became the remedy for so many things. I felt like no matter how hard I searched for God and how much I tried to do all the "right" things, God was a million miles away and wasn't hearing me. I would scream to God for him to take it all away, for him to give me a reason to live. The biggest downturn in my mental health came when I was around 17. My depression had spiralled deeper and deeper into darkness and I found myself attempting to take my life. I was angry at God for every morning I woke up alive still. Why was he allowing me to feel like this? I kept praying to God to show or give me a reason to live. At this point, I was first put on to medication and my family began to realise that all wasn't well with me.

As I began university, I was in full self-destruct mode. I attempted to present myself as a confident happy-go-lucky girl who didn't have a care in the world, when deep down I was tearing myself apart. I continued to pray, asking God for a reason to still be alive, for him to take away my feelings and take me out of the place I was in. I was so desperate for a way out of my life but I just couldn't see my life being any different.

Until one day, when I found out I was pregnant. My head raced with thoughts: *This couldn't be happening to me, what am I meant to do?* Although I began resenting this baby inside me for stopping me from self-destructing, I soon came to realise that now I had a reason to live, and this little baby inside me was my chance for a new start.

Having my daughter gave me a focus, took my mind off of going round in circles and brought a little light to my darkness. I was so desperate to be loved and have someone love only me, and on some level I had found that. Around six months after I had my daughter, life quickly plunged back into deep darkness and I found myself desperate for help.

I was given CBT (cognitive behavioural therapy) for a good few months and put back on to medication. Many situations around me fed my depression and I once again found myself desperate for a way out. I began psychotherapy which lasted around 18 months which made things much harder at times but some days I would see some progress from it. Life felt a little clearer and brighter and things seemed to be going on OK.

I came to accept that depression was always going to be a part of my life, I just needed to somehow carry on with medication and support from those around me. I met my (now) husband and I began to believe that someone could truly love me for me. Despite having someone who loved and cared for me this didn't stop depression having power over my life and the road to life free from depression felt so long still. I felt so ungrateful for having this amazing man who loved me and my daughter and still couldn't find "happiness".

Finally with the help of another round of psychotherapy I found myself being surprised at how well I was coping with life and the changes that were happening. Now, eight years on from first having depression and six years of being on medication, I have finally come off medication and can honestly say that I feel a "happiness" about life. Yes, things are hard sometimes and I have bad days, but I finally have a hope for each day, I look forward to my future, and the rest of my life – something which I haven't done in years.'

'KEEP
ON
TURNING
THE
PAGES'

SANDRA KRING

I read this with such gratitude. This is not someone glossing over the hard times, or smiling with gritted teeth. This is a girl who knows what it is to suffer and yet has come through a great deal of that, stronger and braver for it.

LESSONS FROM THE PAST

One of the largest griefs I have had to deal with was the loss of my innocence that occurred first as a child. I was abused from the age of six until the age of 22 by a number of different men. I cannot remember much before the age of six so it felt for some time as though my whole childhood was marred by those memories.

I have asked God many questions about why he allowed those people access to me and why those things happened. I have, at various times in my life, grieved the childhood I dreamt of and have been sad about the self-image issues, the heartache and the soul-searching that came with those horrible encounters.

It has been a long journey for me to find freedom and I know I am still on the road towards that. But I can honestly tell you that whilst I would never wish such a thing on any young girl, I would be the poorer in my faith and my understanding of life if those things had not happened to me. Most people who meet me now have no idea I have ever had any issues in this area. They are surprised how trusting I am. I do not act, look or sound like a woman who has been abused.

This is because God is a healing God. He doesn't leave us as we are, but takes us to new places of wholeness and completeness in him. I have learnt that beautiful fact many times.

God works for our good, even when what happens to us is bad. He can turn it around.

He has used what men did to me to show me what true love is. He has turned what was meant to harm me into something that has healed me, and healed others.

MAKING SENSE OF ME

At the age of 19 I was working as a steward, moving chairs at a Christian conference in the UK. One evening in the youth venue, the team were inundated with a huge response. I was asked if I was willing to pray with some girls. No one chose who came to speak to me that night. There was no 'pre-interview' to decide the best person. There was no time for all that. I had a queue of girls needing prayer. Everyone did.

But my queue had been handpicked by God. Every single girl that night who came forward and spoke to me had suffered, or was still suffering from a type of abuse that I knew personally. As we prayed together, I sensed God underlining for me part of my life's work. To set the captives free.

Can I suggest something to you?

What you may be going through now might be for someone else's freedom and rescue. You may be struggling through a river of grief that you will one day wade through confidently, taking someone you love with you.

Jesus lets us go through certain things for ourselves, but for others, too.

CAMEL GIRL

Recently I was listening to an album by the amazing worshipper and prayer warrior Sean Feucht. His lyric, 'It's been cloudy for far too long' struck a chord. My life felt very cloudy indeed. I asked God to speak to me and give me a picture or some clue of what he was up to in me. Then He really hit me with something. Do you know what he did? He told me I was a camel!

'Pardon God? Did you just call me a camel?' I asked, not all that pleased at the connotation.

'I did,' I heard back.

'Oh.' I said, not exactly thrilled.

I felt it was right to look up what camels can do and what they are good at. I learnt the following:

Camels are load-bearing animals. Their humps act as reservoirs of fatty tissue that are a source of energy. Their thick coats can withstand harsh sun and strong sand storms. They can go for long periods without water and then drink 100 litres in one go.

They can bear very high temperature rises and falls that would kill other animals. Their gait and wide feet help them move through the sand without getting stuck in it.

Their faeces can be used as a dry fuel to stoke a fire. Their milk is a whole-food, rich in vitamins, minerals and proteins.

They travel at a rate of two or three miles per hour and can carry 500-1000 pounds in weight on their backs. They can keep this up for six to seven hours a day. But they will refuse to carry loads that are not properly balanced.

I found all of that totally fascinating. Suddenly camels didn't seem like a bad thing to be associated with. I began to start to see myself a little differently. If God called me a camel then maybe I *could* bear what he was giving me. Maybe I was trained for this period of drought and famine more than I realised.

Looking back I now see that God very graciously allowed me a season of doubt to strengthen my faith. He allowed me to question my calling in order to underline it. He allowed me to lose what was dear to me in order to realise what was more important.

I am proud to be a camel!

He didn't answer my prayers because they were not in line with his will. He knew that what I needed was not a God I could order around and control but someone bigger than me, wiser than me, with higher ways than mine. He knew I really wanted someone who was sovereign, someone who was in possession of all knowledge and someone who was in control.

The fact is that God is big enough to cope when we doubt him, or fear that he is not there. He is unstintingly kind, generous and fully able to bless us anyway. I don't know the exact day when my trust in God loomed large again but I know it was around the time that I started worshipping him again just in the quiet of my little prayer room, on my own. He was waiting for me, of course. Not with recriminations and the wearied sarcasm of someone greatly let down, expecting more where that came from, but with the open arms of a loving, unchanging father. I started to look at the past few months in a different way. I began to realise that I had not stayed the same; that I had, in fact, grown and changed for the better. I understood some of the wonderful things that God had allowed me to learn as a by-product of my grief.

Looking back, even only to a few weeks ago, I did not believe that was possible. But it is! God can use everything that the enemy plans to harm us to bless us.

POSITIVES OF GRIEF

Here are some things grief can do in you as it has done in me:

1. It can make you more aware of your need for God
2. It can show you new parts of your faith
3. It can make you more compassionate towards others
4. It can make you more aware of the enemy's schemes against you
5. It can make you wiser
6. It can make you more forgiving and trusting
7. It can help you accept yourself more fully
8. It can help you reassess and question your priorities
9. It can bring a family closer together
10. It can bring the reality of heaven nearer
11. It can make you more bold in sharing your faith with others
12. It can make you vulnerable with others and deepen relationships
13. It can make you more determined to live well
14. It can allow you to develop spiritual and emotional maturity
15. It can make your prayer life richer
16. It can allow you to find comfort and truth in God's word
17. It can spark levels of creativity and energy

That's quite a long list.

So be encouraged. God may well be about to do some incredible things in you!

God will work all things together for good. Remember the story of Joseph? At the end in Genesis 50:20 he was able to say to his brothers:

'You intended to harm me, but God intended it for good.'[3]

Your grief will be worked out for your good, too.

LOVE LETTER

A few months after my Mum died, an amazing friend of mine, Emma Pears, sent me this letter. I have asked her permission to print it in full. I think it is one of the most helpful things I have ever read on the subject of grief.

'Someone once described grief to me as an ocean. It is always there, lapping at your feet. Some waves are stronger than others. Then there's the almighty massive wave which comes in every so often and crashes over your head. It comes, often inexplicably, often stealthily and can easily knock you off your feet.

The thing I have found about grief is that there's no easy way through it.

You can't go around it. If you try to, you'll just keep walking and walking, feeling numb till eventually, with no hope of a turning point on the horizon, you have to turn to face it.

You need to take a deep breath. Walk into the water where the current is unpredictable and forceful. You have to keep on walking. Soaked through to skin.

Find restful moments to catch your breath.

Find the times when you've the strength to wade, to lift heavy legs and make progress. To face the pain, embrace it, even.

We are in pain because we love.

To numb the pain delays the inevitable and gives us a pause for relief but we cannot stay there. We must not stay there. For battling on at whatever pace is crucial to move out of the water.

I have learned that when confusion sets in, so must our faith. When we can see clearly, little faith is required. Faith is hope in what we cannot see. When it is dark, that's when faith kicks in. It is not based on feelings. It is not based on answers. It is based on the thread of God running through our DNA which holds us unswervingly to the truth that regardless of circumstances, God is God and God is good!

His will is not always the easy route for us. He never promised it would be. He didn't even provide an easy route for Jesus. Why should we expect one?

Life is messy. It hurts. It brings up questions and rarely provides answers. That is why this life is temporary and heaven is permanent.

In heaven there will be no crying. There is no promise of a life on earth without tears. No promise of ease. That's for heaven. What there is here is a God who cares for us and can comfort us by his Spirit. He knows the pain of living on earth. He knows the confusion. The striving.

I have learned through grief, sickness and pain, the difference between hope and faith. Proverbs says that a "hope deferred makes the heart sick". I get that. Constantly hoping for fruit, for success, for reward, for breakthrough is exhausting. But faith... Faith doesn't wear us out. It builds us up.

I cling on to Psalm 127 which reminds me that it is more about him than me. He doesn't drive me to exhaustion, I do. And if I'm really honest, it's because of my lack of faith. I try to fix things, make things happen. I'm reminded of Abraham trying to have a son his own way by including Hagar into the plan. What a mess!

Have faith. Let your foundation see you through. You are not built on sand. You CAN survive this tidal wave. You are built on The Rock. It hurts.

It's exhausting. The question was never, "Will it rain?" The question is, "When it does rain, what is your foundation: sand or rock?"

It feels never ending, but you are on a journey. Not standing still. People on a journey move from one place to another. Keep moving. Don't stand still. There is no quick fix. No easy answer. Wade in. Wade in and keep moving, because when the water that feels like it will drown you starts to subside, when it becomes knee depth again and then ankle depth, you will find you can run again. You'll be wet from the experience: never the same again. But the weight of wading through currents will subside and you'll feel free to pick up the pace.

There are seasons for everything. The trick is recognising which season you are in and being willing to live it till the season changes.

Be gentle on yourself. Dig deep. Cry much. Eat much. Do what you have to do to keep moving... Don't stand still, don't give up.

People who give up and sit down stay where they are. That's not for you. No short cuts. Bravery and courage are needed, keep moving.

Things will get better.'

ONE YEAR ON

I am writing this one year to the day that Mum died: June 17, 2013.

I feel sad. I miss her. I don't want to talk about it much because I don't want to upset my children. I haven't told them what today is, what it means for me. It didn't feel fair to do that before school.

I am trying to work in the hope that this will help me, but to treat today like an ordinary day feels wrong. It is not ordinary. It is a sacred, painful, wonderful, hopeful and strange day. So many conflicting emotions are vying for top position in my head. I oscillate between wanting to cry then being a lot more peaceful. The children were naughty this morning. Or were they? Was it just my heightened sensitivity today? I don't know. I couldn't bear them arguing because the space in my head felt like I was in church. It was inappropriate for them to be rude.

Today is the anniversary of my Mum no longer being here. I ache inside. Life is so different. I am so different. But I hold her memory like a soft pillow, near to me, gentle against my heart. I am grateful for all I know now that I did not know a year ago. I have journeyed. I have moved on. My trust in God has not diminished but has been set alight. Mum would have approved of that, mightily.

Thank you, Jesus, especially today, for my darling Mumka. I miss you darling,

Moppet x

CHEERS!
THANK YOU!
BONJOUR!

LOSING A FRIEND

'We call that person who has lost his father, an orphan; and a widower that man who has lost his wife. But that man who has known the immense unhappiness of losing a friend, by what name do we call him? Here every language is silent and holds its peace in impotence.'

Joseph Roux[1]

For this chapter, I interviewed a friend of mine, Hannah Lamberth, about her experiences of grief and how it felt to lose her best friend, also called Hannah. I decided to let her tell you this story in her own words.

Q How did you meet your friend Han?

A Hannah and I met at a Christian summer camp in the medical caravan. I have diabetes and she had cystic fibrosis so we both needed care while we were away. We got on like a house on fire straight away. I must have been 13, and she was 12. Sharing a mutual irritation of our respective conditions and a mutual love of anything fun, we formed a strong bond. We liked a lot of the same things and we made each other laugh. Han was hilarious and had a huge zest for life. She lived in Bournemouth and I lived in Southampton, which were only 40 minutes apart on the train. We were inseparable for the few years we knew each other. Undoubtedly, she was my best friend.

Q What was the nature of her condition?

A There is no definitive cure for cystic fibrosis. Han had to have lots of different medications and was a bit of a walking pharmacist. The drugs had the purpose of loosening mucus, expanding her airways, decreasing inflammation and fighting potential lung infections. Han also had to have physio at least twice a day to try and keep her lungs clear. She often had to be on oxygen, too. She couldn't walk a long way. She would have really bad spells when she had to be in a wheelchair and have stays in hospital. Other times she was pretty much like any other teenager.

Q How did she handle her illness?

A She was militant in not letting her condition become her life. She was an exuberant character. Her hair was always a different colour – pink, red, blue, purple. She loved life. She did the things that any other normal teenager would do. A few of us who were close to her learnt how to do her physio which meant she could be a little more independent. She travelled to New Zealand with her sister and even did a sky dive. I think her health insurance for the trip cost way more than the flights and accommodation. She sent me a chocolate bar from NZ which said on it 'P.S. I miss you, from your bestest mate Han.' I still have it.

We always joked about meeting our husbands. If ever we went out we would say to each other 'Husband Opportunity!' It was funny. If she went away she would write me a postcard, 'Not met my husband yet.' I would go to a summer camp and she would ask how the 'husband hunt' was going. For us to be in relationships was something she wanted for me and I wanted for her. In reality, any prospective husband of hers would be widowed young and they would be unlikely to ever have children. But we didn't ever really talk about the reality of marriage. Like any other teenage friends, we invested hours psycho-analysing the here and now and which boys we 'loved' at that time.

Q What was her background like?

A Han had an amazing family. Her Dad was a pastor and her Mum was a teacher. They were a close unit who had a lot of fun together. I loved being with them and always felt like I was part of the family. Her Dad treated me like his own daughter. (At this point Hannah reaches into a memory box and pulls out a card from Han's dad addressed to her. The card says,' Sorry I am not here to welcome you. I have cooked all your meals for whilst I am away. Dad x P.S. Tidy your room before you leave.')

Han spent so much time with her Dad especially and he did a lot of her care. I loved being part of their world and I felt very much at home.

Q What was her prognosis?

A Han's prognosis wasn't great. Sufferers of CF can live until around the age of 30 I think. When you are 15, that age seems a million miles away. Hannah was well aware of this and we did talk about it but we were so young. Even when you have a life-threatening condition, you still feel all the invincibility of being a teenager. We just lived day to day. She was a Christian and she had this 'No Fear!' policy on death. Part of that was her amazing faith and part of it was the way her parents had raised her, to be fearless with Jesus.

Q What were the first indicators that something was wrong?

A Around Christmas time Hannah picked up a chest infection. She had these fairly frequently and had always pulled through them before so although serious, her hospital admission wasn't a massive concern. But she got progressively worse. The hospital started to talk about the possibility of a heart and lung transplant. Han had never wanted a transplant. I remember her telling me that she would feel as though she wouldn't be truly 'herself' with someone else's heart.

Q When did you realise how serious it was?

A One day during the time Han was in hospital, I went to my sixth form college as usual in Southampton. I had been in contact with Hannah's family and knew she was really sick. As I got the bus home it went past the train station and something made me get out and get on a train. I texted Han's sister and asked if I could visit her. She was in Poole Hospital. Her sister texted me back and warned me that she didn't look like herself at all. Looking back, I don't think anyone apart from family was allowed to see her. They all knew she was near the end.

I was shocked when I went into her room. She was normally a tiny, less-than-five-foot girl because of her condition. But she had ballooned and her face was swollen from the many steroids she was on. She squeezed my hand so she knew I was there. I was only allowed five minutes with her. On the train home, the reality of potentially never seeing her again hit me. But there was still hope. The following morning, she was being driven to the Royal Brompton Hospital in London which specialises in heart and lung transplant. Her family had given the decision over to God and prayed that he would do his will.

Han died really early the next morning, hours before she was meant to be driven to get her new heart. It was seven weeks after New Year's Eve, February 20. Han, my lovely 17-year-old best friend was dead.

Q How did you react?

A This was my first real experience of God taking someone when you don't think they should go. She had been in hideous pain for years and her life had been cut painfully short. I asked a lot of questions and wondered why he had taken her then, not earlier, or later.

Looking back I know more of God and understand that there is a very precise and perfect timing to death. Only he understands why he takes someone, or leaves someone on earth longer. We may never grasp why.

I believe that there is a period of intimacy between a person and God during the very last days, hours and even minutes of their life that is so personal and so private. We are not the deciders of the date of death and have to simply trust God. I think she had an amazing experience of God in those last few days.

201

Q What was her funeral like?

A The service was packed to overflowing. They just couldn't get everyone in. There was an amazing time of sung worship with a great band. The funeral itself was incredibly emotional. I can remember people literally wailing out loud. The family decided to do four reflections about her from different people. I did the one on friendship. I remember feeling so privileged that out of all her friends they had chosen me to speak. Han was one of those people that lots of people would call their best friend. It confirmed for me my place in their family and showed me they understood what I had meant to Han, and what she had meant to me. I steeled myself. My resilience kicked in. I spoke as strongly as I could.

Q How did Han's death affect your faith?

A I never became angry at God. But I did become very angry about the number of prophesied healings on earth that had been spoken over her. I was angry at the way those good intentions had such disastrous consequences. Those kind words turned out not to be kind at all. They gave false hope to her family and her loved ones. They gave false hope to me.

It makes me very cautious about healing ministry now. Done in the wrong way it can do a phenomenal amount of damage. It taught me a valuable lesson. You can never put your hope in healing. You have to put your hope in God. Our hope has always got to be in him and never in what he can do. Our hope can't be in our circumstances. In a strange way Han's death heightened my understanding of God's goodness. He always knows. He always loves. He is always good.

But my faith took a battering and the spiritual grief I felt was very real. I was asking God a lot of questions. How do I fit my faith into this? My understanding of God was well-rooted and grounded because of my parents and the biblical upbringing they had given me but it wasn't as established and developed as I had thought. I think it was fairly weak at that time. I was 18. I liked having fun. I liked partying. Han's death brought me to a massive crossroads. Is it worth it? Is it worth being a Christian if it is this hard? Are the spiritual questions I am going through ever going to be answered? Should I just renounce my faith?

Being a Christian almost made my grief harder. People inundated me with cards, words, and verses but I was numb. I didn't feel

'THE
DARKER
THE
NIGHT,
THE
BRIGHTER
THE
STARS'

DOSTOYEVSKY

anything. I couldn't access any of it. For about three years after her death I struggled with my faith a great deal. I lived by the principle that God is good all the time but that Christians are idiots! I didn't do a lot of praying. There was always a connection to him but not necessarily to others who loved him. I felt like I was always touching fingertips with God but not much more. It was as though I was saying: ' I know you are good, I just don't know how to make that work in my own life.'

Q What was living without your friend like in those early days?

A My grief was hard and physical. I remember sobbing and weeping for the first few days. The physical heaviness and the core of pain in my body was immense. It felt horrible.

At the time, there was a song out by Enrique Iglesias called 'Hero.' The words of that used to get to me and make me cry. I would sit and look through old photos of Han, wishing I was back in that world again.

I felt guilt, too, that I just had diabetes and she got dealt CF. I wished we could have traded places.

'What is dying?

A ship sails and I stand watching till she fades on the horizon and someone at my side says, "She is gone". "Gone where?" Gone from my sight, that is all. She is just as large as when I saw her. The diminished size and total loss of sight is in me, not in her. Just at that moment, when someone at my side says, "She is gone," there are others who are watching her coming and other voices take up a glad shout, "Here she comes!"

That is dying.'

Bishop Charles Henry Brent (written on a card given to Hannah at the time of the funeral)

Q How did you grieve?

A It sounds like a cliché, but I felt like the bottom had fallen out of my world. I felt caught between two worlds, Hannah, her family and our friends in Bournemouth and my other friends and family back home. Suddenly these two worlds separated. People attempted to console me but they didn't know what I had lost.

I felt misunderstood. Many people had no idea how close we had been.

They knew me but they hadn't known her. So they couldn't grieve with me. And because they couldn't grieve with me I felt angry at them. People were only trying to help but in my grief, I became irrational. I was so hurt that no one seemed to understand how I felt.

Q What happened after Han died?

A Ten years later it is easy to sum up three years in a sentence. But those were tough times for me. I suffered from a complete loss of concentration. My brain just couldn't hold information. It was strange. As a result, I totally failed my A Levels. But I didn't actually care that much. I just wanted to be with my friends and have fun. In part, this was a result of my grief. Normal things like exams just didn't seem so important anymore. Other friends of mine who had known Han grieved in an extreme way. One of them even turned to drinking heavily. I didn't realise the extent to which she was struggling. I would recognise the signs now but at the time, I didn't see it properly for what it was.

I went to see a GP soon after Han died. It had been two or three months and I knew I was not coping brilliantly. He was really helpful. He was a Christian and a friend of my parents. He even asked permission to pray with me as part of the consultation. He put me on anti-depressants for a while. But I didn't like being on them because I hated feeling nothing. Counselling was talked about at that stage, but I took myself off the pills and I never went back. I decided to just carry on, on my own.

I now know that God works for the good of those who love him and so even in that period of my life where for seven months I didn't do any work and failed my exams, he still had an incredible plan for me.

Q How did your family handle your A Level results?

A University was the thing our family did. We are just one of those families where everyone goes on to higher education. I wanted to go to Bath but of course, I didn't get in. I ended up going to UCE In Birmingham. It felt like a real reject university, like a recycling bin for failed students and I stayed for a total of ten weeks. All I was doing was going out, trying to have fun, without succeeding very much. I moved back home. I got a job temping and then worked in a call centre for a while. This just fuelled my party lifestyle. But I think I was fairly miserable deep down.

Q What did you do next?

A Somehow I signed up to do a five-month evangelistic training course called Xcelerate with The Message Trust in Manchester. I think I had decided that I had to immerse myself in Christianity if I was going to make things work. I got on to the course but nearly got kicked off a couple of times, for not towing the line. I was a very difficult customer at that time!

We were only allowed home for two weekends in the five months. But I went home the first weekend I was there – and many weekends after that, too. I took the attitude of, 'I am paying for this! I can do what I like.' I felt angry and often misunderstood. I had no idea that this was part of my grieving. I am only realising as I am speaking to you now that it was all connected. I started the course in August 2004 and at that point I hadn't had any grief counselling or prayer. I still haven't really. They didn't know why I was messed up. But I definitely was. I was hard work for them!

Q Did you receive any support?

A I decided to become part of an Eden team with a charity called The Message Trust in an area of Manchester called Swinton. I lived on a rough estate and it was a hard time for me. I believed in the idea of Eden, living out the gospel in forgotten areas, but I had not got over my own sense of loss. Living in a harsh environment when you are lacking grace is not a great idea. People had high expectations of me because I was living out this role as part of this full time Christian ministry but a lot of issues in me were still very raw.

I would have benefitted from counselling or Christian prayer ministry, I know that now. But I didn't know it at the time. I was still functioning. I was still in relationship. I felt like I was OK. I blamed how I was feeling on being 20 but actually I think now it was a lot more closely linked to my sense of loss than I knew.

Q What is Han's legacy in your life?

A Her death made me aware of the huge degrees of subjectivity in life. I learnt that there isn't a 'standard human response' to anything. Your experiences, the way that you are brought up, the relationships you have... all of these are a factor in how your respond to things, especially to adversity. When I hear how someone has dealt negatively with something, I try to work out why they might have done that. I try to see the best in the person. Even when someone commits a horrific crime, my mind says 'How did that person get to the point where this became acceptable to them?'

It has made me aware that we don't just have a responsibility to teach our kids right and wrong, but we need to equip them to deal with emotional hardship, too. I know I am relatively 'baggage free' in comparison to others. But I have still had my issues to work through. You can't protect your children from everything that might hurt them. It is much better to equip them to deal with problems and how to walk through them when they happen.

Her life made me want to find joy in as much as I can and to bring happiness into people's lives. I want my daughter to remember her childhood fondly. I prize her happiness highly and I want to help make her full of joy.

It has also made me realise the value of community. My relationship with

Han wasn't just with her. When we go into intensive friendships that are based on only two people, that can be fragile and, if and when it goes wrong, it is horrific. Jesus understood the value of friendship in the context of community. I love my friends dearly but I don't have one best friend any more. I hold my friendships loosely and as open-handedly as I can. I have amazing friends, people that are more like family to me really, but I don't want one exclusive friend any more.

In some ways, I still live with the mantra of 'God is good and Christians can be idiots!' It helps me to forgive people and think the best of them. My expectations of people are very realistic and I try not to feel that people owe me anything.

Q How has knowing Han impacted how you run your own family now?

A I was privileged to have a really intimate insight into the way another family worked. Because I went to stay with Han a lot, I saw big chunks of their family time together. It wasn't a local friendship where I just went for tea. I would stay for days at a time and be part of everything they did. That insight has changed how I parent and how we raise our little girl.

207

My family are great but they operate very differently to how Han's family lived. Han's Mum and Dad were open about everything. This was great training for when I became part of my husband Dave's family, who are very similar. Han's family had this sense of fun and you would laugh at every meal time. They were very warm and tactile and would offer you a drink with a hand on your shoulder. There was lots of hugging. Every day Hannah knew she was loved. Sensitive subjects were talked about easily. My family were amazing too but more formal and confidential. This is good because I know if I told something to my mum it would not go anywhere. It was private and kept under wraps. But nothing was taboo in Han's family. Everything was out in the open. I am very grateful for the two contrasts and the two types of experience of family.

At this point in our conversation, Hannah got out her memory box and began to show me some of the items inside.

Q Do you ever go through this memory box now?

A Not really. There are only a small handful of people that I shared that part of my life with. It feels like a long time ago. There were funny sayings that we had. For some reason, I seem to get on well with people who enjoy mimicking foreign accents. One of our little sayings was 'Cheers! Thank you! Bonjour!' It appears on loads of the stuff she has written me. It was just one of those little things that becomes a catchphrase in friendships.

I am still in touch with her sister a little bit. I did keep in contact with her parents for a while. But I moved up to Birmingham in the September and then the following August I moved to Manchester. Over time they weren't in my everyday world any more and so our friendship naturally dwindled a bit. Then they moved away and so we didn't have one place where we had always been together. That said, Facebook is a wonderful thing and I love seeing photos and snapshots of what they're up to.

Q How are you now?

A I am well. I have decided to stop working at our church. I was part of the leadership team for over two years and had responsibility for pastoral care. After the recent death of my mother-in-law, Denise, life changed rather dramatically for our family. We felt that we wanted to spend more time with Dave's dad, supporting him and just hanging out with him. We have decided to move into the same house and live as a multi-generational unit. I think it will be fun!

The last few months of caring for Denise as she was ill and helping the family through that have been tiring, especially trying to work at the same time. We have become really aware that there are many others in and outside of our church family who need us to be there in a practical sense for them. I don't want to be rushed off my feet writing emails anymore. I want to be sharing the love of Jesus with precious people in need over a coffee. I think Han would totally approve of my decision to rush less and care more. Plus more chatting, coffee and of course cake would definitely get her seal of approval!

PROMISES OF LIFE

As I wrote up Hannah's story, I was reminded of the amazing verses in Joel 2:25–26:

> '*I will restore to you the years that the swarming locust has eaten, the hopper, the destroyer, and the cutter, my great army, which I sent among you. You shall eat in plenty and be satisfied, and praise the name of the Lord your God, who has dealt wondrously with you. And my people shall never again be put to shame.*'[4]

I love the truth that God will restore us and fill us with good things.

The phrase and promise that God is someone 'who has dealt wondrously with you...' has struck me hard for Hannah. It feels both very obvious and significant to me that God has his hand on her life. The way he treats her is wondrous because he has beautiful plans for her. Nothing she has gone through is wasted. I know she will never be put to shame for the choices she is making because she is basing her life around the purposes of God.

What about you?

Do you know this truth for yourself?

Have you felt like Hannah at any stage of your grief or are you still in the midst of something similar?

Take heart and be encouraged. Even without counselling, prayer ministry or long doses of anti-depressants, God can be your 'portion'. He and He alone is enough to bring you out and bring you through. He will deal wondrously with you, too.

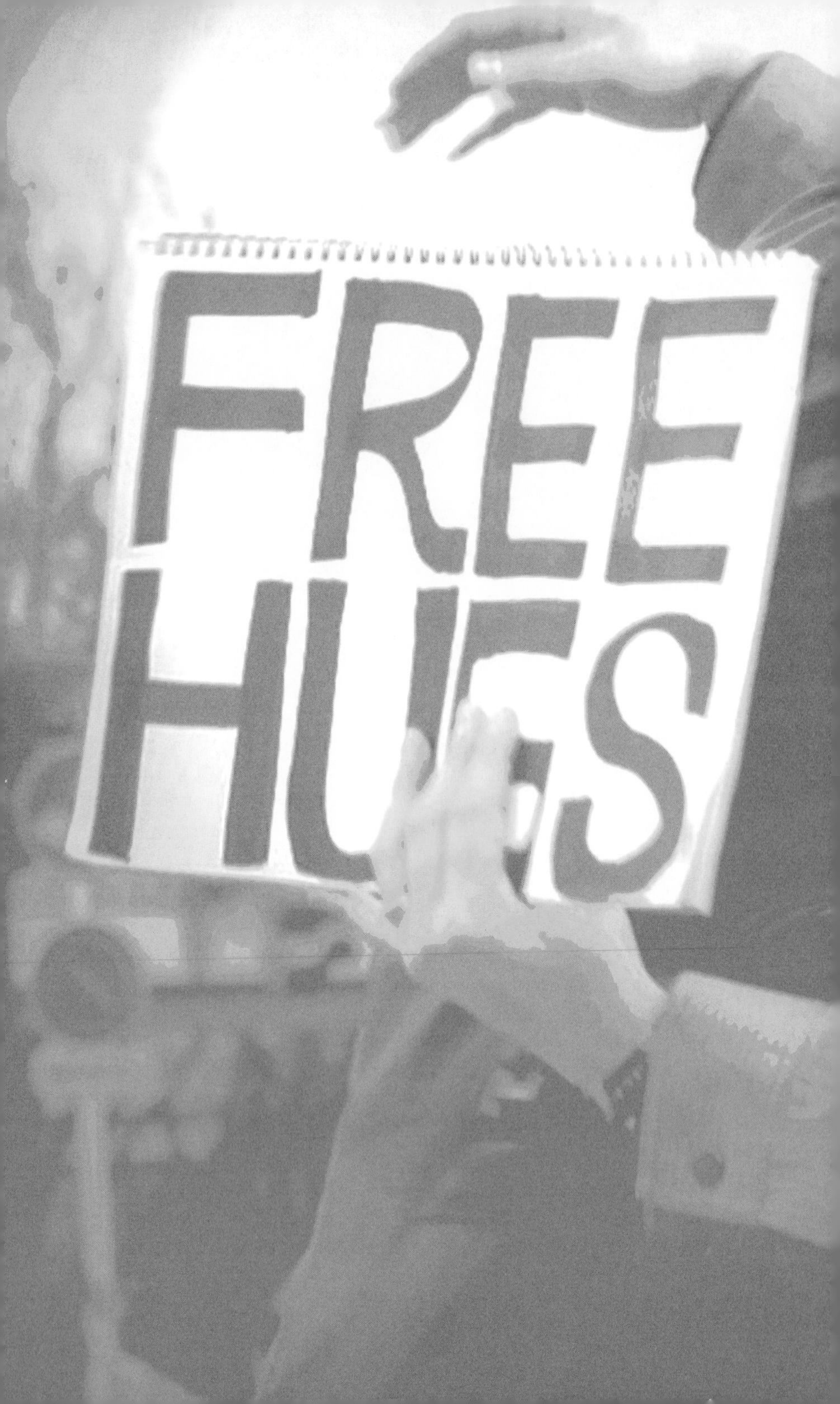
FREE

HANDLE
WITH CARE
COMFORTING OTHERS

'The renowned Bayeux Tapestry, tells the story among other things, of the Battle of Hastings. In one panel King Harold is seen poking his troops in the rear end, with an arrow, urging them into battle. The inscription under this image is best translated as, "Harold comforteth his troops."

To comfort, in the ancient world, was not to make comfortable. It was to encourage, to spur on, to urge towards battle and perhaps death.

The comforter who comes to us brings strength and a call to action. He comes to piece us together, to equip us, to make us all that we should be.'

Gerard Kelly, Twitturgies[1]

I once went into a department store for some new makeup. As I ambled over to the concession of one of the more well-known brands I was horrified to see a young girl with a streaked orange face, black, thickly-drawn eyebrows, bright red matt lipstick and so much mascara it looked as though her eyes had had surgical implants at the expense of an unfortunate spider's legs. Her dyed white-blonde hair was piled up on top of her head like a strangely rolled rug. I quickly changed my mind and scarpered – there was no way 'Little Miss Orang-utan' was giving me cosmetic advice.

I spotted an older lady on a different counter who looked far more gentle. Her makeup was subtle, but beautiful. It did not scream, 'Notice me! Fear my enormous fake lashes! Smell my peroxide!' I wandered over to her stand and started up a conversation. Her voice matched her makeup, soothing and soft. She looked natural and not as though she was going to grab me by the neck and daub thick dollops of Fake Bake on my face. I chose her.

Grief makes us choose certain people. We will search for those who can offer us natural comfort and make us feel at home. Those who have gone through the same things we are going through can make the best companions on the journey. We don't want the fake 'loud' stuff. We want the real deal. We want to be treated gently. As with a fragile parcel, we might feel like labelling ourselves, 'This way up! Handle with care!'

People who have suffered some kind of grief often know what others in their same situation need. They can be the best helpers, although they may assume you will react in the same way to them – which you may not.

TALKING ABOUT GRIEF

I was once on a motorway and the dreaded 'queue ahead' sign appeared above the carriageway. I groaned (in a very holy way, of course) because I hate being stuck in traffic. The cars slowed to 50, then 40, then 30 and then total standstill.

I guessed there was an accident up ahead and I was right. But, incredibly it was not on my side of the road. Rubbernecking (gawping at the scene of an accident) was what had slowed everyone down. The tell-tale debris of two smashed up cars was strewn across the road on the other side. Flashing police lights and ambulance crews were all busy working. The backlog of traffic was miles long. Grief may not have happened to you recently, but perhaps to someone you love deeply. It may have had the impact of slowing everything and everyone around that person or family down. You may just be watching the debris across the road and not feel able to help much.

But there are some ways in which you can get involved. This chapter is not just for people who are grieving, but for those caring for them.

If you are meeting up with someone who has lost a loved one and is struggling to come to terms with that, here are some things you can do:

1. Ask God for guidance about when to speak and what to say.

2. Be a good listener. Don't judge what is said. Grief can make people say things they won't feel and wouldn't dream of saying in a few weeks or months, but they certainly mean them fully at the time. Some of those things can be disturbing – 'I don't want to live

any more!' or 'How can I carry on?' Remember that Romans 12:15 says, 'Weep with those who weep.' At times you may be on the receiving end of a grieving person who is very angry. This can be hard to hear but it is much healthier for them to express this out loud to you, than to keep it in and let if fester. If you feel hurt or damaged by what someone has said in your hearing, ask someone you trust to pray for you.

3. Try to avoid black and white platitudes. Allow the person to express their grief without suggesting that they should 'cheer up' or 'be joyful in the Lord.' This could give the impression you are questioning or belittling the person's spirituality or journey. It can also just be plain insensitive and uncaring!

4. Don't be too pushy or preachy. If the person indicates any kind of openness, pray and share precious scriptures with them, but always be careful as to the length of any conversation – making sure you are listening more than talking. (Yup! Talking to myself there!)

BE THERE

It was a Sunday. My husband Jon and the kids had gone to church. We were trying to keep things as normal as possible for them. I went to my parents' home where my Dad, eldest brother, middle brother and his wife had all gathered. Only an hour later, my Mum died.

I rang Jon straightaway, just as he was walking into the cinema where our church currently meets. After checking I was OK, he handed the phone to Anthony, our church leader, who prayed for me. I can't tell you how precious that prayer was and how upheld I felt. Just seconds after my Mum had 'gone to glory,' someone who loved me and cared for me as my pastor was celebrating her arrival in heaven and sharing in our devastating loss.

His being there for us in that immediate moment was so valuable.

It felt like it was a message from God himself.

'ALL SEPARATION IS TEMPORARY FOR BELIEVERS'

UNKNOWN

The following day, another pastor from church came round to comfort me.

She stood with me in my kitchen and held me so tightly that breathing wasn't much of an option. She told me she loved me and spoke the words of Psalm 23 fiercely and fondly over me. My memory of that week is very hazy, but I have no problem remembering how she treated me. She rang me many times in the few weeks that followed and checked up on me in regular texts. She took me out for coffee and breakfast and we laughed and cried together.

The elders of the church were similarly kind, and the ones I know well showed immediate care and support.

Especially if you are a leader or elder of a church, how you handle the grief or loss of a person in your church community will be remembered forever. It is because in that moment, time stands totally, achingly still. It is a gaping hole and you can help fill it. If you ring or visit or email or send a card, that person will treasure it. If you are not available, or don't send someone who is, that will give a message to the grieving person about their place in your heart and in the wider church family.

That's a message no one wants to send, or receive.

Whoever you are – sister, leader, friend, neighbour – if you are not already there when a death happens, get there. Show your presence by phone, text, email or visit, as soon as you can. Don't leave a gap because you don't know what to say. Words often aren't what's needed anyway. Ring and leave a message saying you are sorry. Say anything. Just don't say nothing.

One of my dear friends from our church back in Kent where we used to live, rang me and left a long, rambling message on my phone soon after Mum's death. She was clearly crying and was almost entirely incoherent. But it made me feel so loved that she was grieving WITH me. Nothing is more important than not feeling alone after a loss.

'All separation is temporary for believers.'

Unknown

GOD – THE COMFORTER

As I quoted in an earlier chapter, God is 'the God of all comfort, who comforts us in all our troubles.'[2] The word 'all' is important here. There is not a human emotion that he doesn't fully understand and there is not a sensation he cannot change. He is ALL sufficient.

I read an amazing quote recently somewhere that said, 'The future is as bright as the promises of God.' If we grasped that in all its life-affirming power, whatever we were facing, things would look very different, wouldn't they?

As a Christian of more than 36 years, I can say that God is real, that the promises of scripture are true and that there is life through and after loss. Not because I have read those things in a book, but because of having lived them.

In the wonderful book of Revelation, God offers an amazing word about our grief:

> 'Then I saw a new heaven and a new earth, for the first heaven and the first earth had passed away ... And I heard a loud voice from the throne saying, 'Now the dwelling of God is with men, and he will live with them. They will be his people, and God himself will be with them and be their God. He will wipe every tear from their eyes. There will be no more death or mourning or crying or pain, for the old order of things has passed away' (Revelation. 21:1a, 3–4)[3]

What an amazing day that will be for you and for me!

GIFTS AND PRACTICAL HELP

In the midst of a crisis, especially in church circles, people can flock around being all pastoral and busy. There is a flurry of cards, meals, babysitting and flowers but it is all a bit of a whirlwind. After the funeral is over and the family members are gone, it can go very flat. And very quiet.

After Mum died we were given around 30 beautiful bunches of flowers.

I hated the sight of cut flowers for a long time after that! They just reminded me of her death. I have read other books on grief where this is a similar feeling for those in pain.

Perhaps flowers aren't always the best things to send. Some people love them, but, well, think about it, flowers die! There are more inventive ways to bless friends at a time like this. It may be that a grocery shop or a store gift card would be more useful. Perhaps a photograph frame, a CD or a special book.

A few days after the funeral is a good time to check up on the grieving person. Texting or emailing is a lovely thing to do, but nothing beats just showing up and leaving a meal, or some other small thoughtful gift.

After my Grandma died, an amazing friend of mine left a bag on our doorstep. Inside it were two meals, bubble bath, tissues, a magazine and some hot chocolate. But what was really precious was that each gift had a label stuck to it... 'For when you feel like crying...' ' For when you need a hug... ' 'For when you are aching...' I had been on high alert and coping mode. I dissolved into tears when I opened the bag. It was just what I needed and was such an incredible blessing. It made me suddenly think about my own needs.

But I would expect nothing else from this lady. She truly knows the pain of grief in all its depth and awfulness. She and her husband had the enormous sadness of losing a baby boy during the final days of pregnancy. Two years on, their grief still looms large and their lives have been utterly changed by the loss of their lovely little one. She gave from a heart that really knew what I would need. And she was spot on.

Some people require practical help with child care, cooking, legalities and funeral arrangements. If you are the sort of person who can do these things, always offer. They may not be needed, but in my experience it is always better to check.

Recently I spoke to my friend Dave whose mum had died two months previously. I asked him how people had cared for them as a family during the time of his Mum's illness and after her death. Here's what he said:

'We were given so many gifts. Our church friends totally carried us.

We didn't know what each day was going to bring, what we would need or how we would feel, but God did. We got sent cinema vouchers when we needed a break. People offered to have our daughter at just that right time. It was more than just church being church, it was godly gifts given by human hands. It was truly mind-blowing. What was so incredible was that people anticipated our needs before we had them. We had so much food made for us that we ended up giving doggy bags to the health visitors!

Then, to top it all off, on the day of Mum's funeral we were given an envelope. Inside it was a sizable cheque from a large number of people at church, giving us the means to go on holiday. Only five days after the funeral, we flew out to Portugal as a family with my Dad for some much needed respite. It made a massive difference to how we grieved those first few weeks. That holiday helped us move on to the next stage and we are so grateful we had that time out together.

And as for the day of the funeral itself, I honestly look back on it now as almost like a wedding. We had so much to be thankful for. Mum was safe in heaven and we were able to celebrate that with so many people – those who know and trust God and those who have never made that step.'

'There is nothing like the local church when it's working right. Its beauty is indescribable. Its power is breathtaking. Its potential is unlimited. It comforts the grieving and heals the broken in the context of community. It builds bridges to seekers and offers truth to the confused. It provides resources for those in need and opens its arms to the forgotten, the downtrodden, the disillusioned. It breaks the chains of addictions, frees the oppressed, and offers belonging to the marginalised of this world. Whatever the capacity for human suffering, the church has a greater capacity for healing and wholeness.'

Bill Hybels[4]

TO VISIT, OR NOT TO VISIT?

Sometimes people won't want 'actual' visitors straight away. To be honest, I dreaded it when people came to see me. I did not want to be 'seen' – not really. I only wanted my very close friends and family near me. But things that people dropped off for me, little things sent in the post, or messages on my phone, all really blessed me and helped me feel loved.

Others say they find it hugely comforting to be surrounded by an army of friends. We are all different. Don't be afraid to ask what is needed and then aim to provide it.

BE SENSITIVE

Here are three important little words: don't assume anything. Everyone grieves differently. Don't be afraid to talk to the person about what they need. Nine times out of ten, especially in the early days, they simply may not know. I lost count of the amount of times I said that ('I just don't know!') to people around me after Mum died. But ask anyway.

And don't just ask, 'How are you?' Ask things like, 'If you could do anything today, what would it be?' Questions like that give the grieving person the chance to think about their own desires and needs and what would help them. And that gives you a chance to make it happen.

One girl going through grief really surprised me one day by saying, 'I want you to tell me the story of how you went to the wrong country on the wrong day. I need a good laugh!' Sometimes a grieving person doesn't want to talk about their loved one. They need taking out of themselves – to remember that there are other topics of conversation and that life can be funny.

At one funeral I remember, I went up to a family member, gave him a hug and asked him how he was doing. I expected a typically doleful reply. Instead he smiled and said, 'Oh well. It's a day out for the family, isn't it?' What he needed from me in that moment wasn't sympathy, but empathy. He needed a laugh and some help to get through the awkwardness and strangeness of the moment.

Not so long ago, I was chatting to the lady who waxes my legs about her family and the way they 'do' funerals. She told me that they have a very dark sense of humour and that when her uncle was cremated, they played the song 'Relight my fire!' Not everyone wants a sombre funeral.

Each to their own!

At other times, the thing people most need is a good, hard cry. That can be overwhelming for some. We can feel uncomfortable with open displays of deep emotion. But this may be exactly what is required.

The Bible is clear that we should 'mourn with those who mourn' (Romans 12:15). Many times when I have been praying with someone who is really battling grief, my eyes have filled with tears for them. The Holy Spirit has given me a share in their sorrow. Perhaps this has happened for you too.

Funny story… I once went for psycho-sexual therapy at a well-known counselling agency for couples. Now, I am sure that most of their counsellors are great and that I just got a duff one… but the following is totally true.

I started to share some of my story of abuse with the lady in question and she got more and more distraught. A few minutes later she left the room in tears and came back with a large box of tissues. I spent the rest of the session reassuring her that she would be OK and that perhaps she needed to find someone to talk to about her reaction to my past as it was clearly difficult for her to hear.

Who was counselling who?!

I went home feeling more than a little odd. Her reaction had been unprofessional and unhelpful, to say the least. I rang my best friend to ask if I should go back and her answer included words like 'barge pole' and 'don't touch with'.

Showing emotion when someone else is sad is totally appropriate – as long as you don't totally fall apart on them and start to make it about you.

You may be tempted to think, 'I don't want to get them to talk about it; it'll only make them feel worse!' Often, though, it is a huge comfort to talk about the person we miss. It keeps the memory real and that helps us feel as though we are honouring them. It can also really help us to know that someone else valued the person we are grieving, too.

It may sound silly, but just starting to get used to talking about someone in the past tense takes practice. But the process is needed, and helpful.

WATCH YOUR WORDS

It's hard to know what to say to someone who is grieving. It might be easier to remember what *not* to say. For example, I think it is always wise to avoid saying, 'I know how you feel.' Because we absolutely don't! We may know something of what they have experienced, but that is nothing like being in their heads and feeling their emotions. So I would never say it.

I remember hearing the awful story of one poor young mum whose child had died at birth being told by a truly thoughtless lady,

'I know just how you feel. My cat died last week.'

Oh. My. Word.

Other things NOT to say to a grieving person are:

'Time is a healer.'
'You're not looking your best.'
'Have you been left a lot of money?'
'You'll find someone else.'
'You always wanted to go round the world/start knitting classes/take up kick boxing (delete as applicable) – now is your chance!'
'Don't cry.'
'I will always be here for you.' (Because no one can promise that.)

Don't even quote whole Bible verses 'at' them. Romans 8:28 is true and amazing at all times, but may not be what is needed when the wound of grief is so fresh and raw. And the person you say it to may be tempted to attack you with their golf clubs/slow cooker/patio chairs.

What I did find very helpful were texts telling me I was loved and precious, encouraging me and lifting me up to the Lord.

One such, was this EPIC one from a dear friend:

'I am so sorry to hear that it's such a hard time for you. I will definitely pray. Be encouraged that the Holy Spirit led Jesus into the wilderness; that both Father God and Satan had plans for Jesus during that time, but Jesus won the battle, fighting with the TRUTH and came out the other side EMPOWERED by the Holy Spirit.

I really believe God is saying that this is a season; a season where God is building new capacity in you and I know without a shadow of a doubt that though God may ask different things of you during this season your heart for him and your spirit being obedient (even when your flesh doesn't always feel like it) will take you to a whole new level of authority in the heavenly realms...

I am agreeing with the whole of heaven that God has amazing things in store for you and your family and that as you allow yourself to be weak and broken Yahweh will be your strength. I agree with heaven that LIFE and WHOLENESS comes out of brokenness and sacrifice. I agree with heaven that God is Jehovah Jireh and that you will look back and count this trial a blessing and that you will let perseverance finish its work so that you may be mature and complete, not lacking anything.'

That was a pretty good text to receive I can tell you (and I have actually edited it to make it a good bit shorter! Ha!) But on the day I got it, I was so low and so sad I couldn't take it in. Not at all. I knew it was a significant one and kept it on my phone to re-read later. I am so glad I did because I can now look back and see how God has started to answer her faithful prayers. But I got that text six months ago and am only just seeing how it makes sense.

So, tell the grieving person you are praying for her or him. More than that, actually *do it*. Make a note of what the Lord tells you to pray for. Be encouraged that even if you don't know what to say, the Holy Spirit is interceding on your behalf with groans too deep for words (Romans 8:26).

Written prayers are very valuable things. I encourage you to take some time to write out a prayer for your grieving friend. It is something they may come back to time and time again in the coming months and years. As I think I will with my friend's one.

Perhaps you don't feel able to do this and feel that perhaps it wouldn't be appropriate for the person you are caring for. Instead try saying something like:

'I can only try to imagine how you must be feeling.'
'I care for you.'
'I want you to know that I love you deeply.'
'I am available for you today.'

'Call me if I can do anything" is a lovely thing to say to someone who is handling life well. But to a person in grief, that can be an unhelpful phrase because it puts the onus on them having to organise something.

Wherever possible, try to take the initiative instead. Offer to cook, clean, babysit, walk the dog, care for the children, or just sit and answer the phone.

GOD THE HEALER

You and I are not Jesus. We may be his hands and feet, but we are not able to do all he does. With this in mind, we must recognise our own limitations and remember that God is the one who 'heals the brokenhearted and binds up their wounds' (Psalm 147:3) not us.

We should do all we can do to comfort others in pain, but we can't do what only God can do. Sometimes he wants to get us, and our friends, to a place where we are truly leaning on him and him alone. So we must not get in his way!

COMFORTING THE DYING

Sometimes we may get the privilege of being with someone in their last days or moments on earth. I think it is wise not to pretend they look well or are going to recover. If someone has come to terms with their destiny and you come in, spouting and shouting the story of Lazarus at them, or rebuking the spirit of death, or talking about a YouTube clip where the dead are being raised, they aren't going to thank you for it. Remember that Lazarus was raised from the dead, but he eventually died again! Everyone dies. (OK. Except Elijah and Enoch... and they are both in heaven!)

Some people in their last days want to talk about heaven, their funeral and practical things about their home and possessions. Jesus was no exception. He often spoke to the disciples about what life would be like in heaven.

When my Mum was dying I found it helped her if I wrote her wishes down, giving them the credence they deserved. She felt calmer and reassured because I was making a note of things she wanted me to remember. It will also help you and others to make a note of things at that time, as your mind can play tricks on you afterwards. Grief can make you tired and make your memory incredibly woolly.

Give people a chance to talk about their actual death if they want to. If you ask them, most Christian people aren't afraid of dying but are actually quite unnerved about the moment of death itself. Talking about it and praying with them can reassure them. Remind them about times in their life when God has proved himself to them, or to you, talk about the certainty of heaven, and assure them you will meet them there.

> 'I do not fear death. I had been dead for billions and billions of years before I was born, and had not suffered the slightest inconvenience from it.'
>
> Mark Twain

THE MOMENT ITSELF

I have been with a number of people at the moment of their death. Each time I have prayed away any fear in myself or in them. Death can be totally peaceful for those dying and for those with them.

What if the person you are visiting does not know Jesus and you do? What can you say then?

If you are a Christian, don't be afraid to be honest about your faith. People can be incredibly receptive on their death bed in a way they have never been before in their active lifetime.

Tell them what you believe about God and eternity unashamedly. If you sense any hostility to your words, close your mouth and open your heart instead. They can't stop you praying silently, so carrying on doing that!

My Dad was able to pray with his own father as he was dying and had the real privilege of praying him into the kingdom. As you may remember, Jesus comforted the thief on the cross next to Him that he would join Him in paradise.

God can pluck people from one destiny to another at the very last minute.

SELF HELP

COMFORTING
YOURSELF

It might be a strange concept to grasp, but I believe that the best person to look after you during a period of grief is actually you. (With the help of the Holy Spirit, of course!)

The day I fully realised this fact, I began to take control of my own healing and care and started to see some real changes in my life.

Being kind to yourself, allowing yourself some time and space, is actually more beneficial than we might realise. In a recent article in 'Well,' a health blog on The New York Times website, Tara Parker-Pope writes, 'Research suggests that giving ourselves a break and accepting our imperfections may be the first step toward better health. People who score high on tests of self-compassion have less depression and anxiety, and tend to be happier and more optimistic.'

Whenever you're anxious, sad or overwhelmed or simply need truth and comfort, it can help to have a collection of practical and healthy tools to turn to.

THINGS TO DO TO COMFORT YOURSELF

Here are some things that I have found SO helpful in the last few months:

1. 'Eat' a short promise of Scripture
There are so many amazing promises of God in the Bible that we need to get into our spirits in order to handle what life throws at us. This means we can't just read a verse once and hope it settles in our hearts. We have to do more.

Many years ago, I had a mentor who was an elderly Jesuit priest. His practice when we met was to teach me other ways of communicating with God. I totally recommend a style of Bible reading called 'Lectio Divina' (Latin for 'divine reading') which he passed on to me. Lectio is an ancient and very helpful method of biblical prayer first formed by monastic communities. There are now specific websites dedicated to this style of worship which are very good quality. No other style of Bible reading has blessed me more in my Christian life than this and I can't recommend it strongly enough. Here is how to do it:

Before you start, get comfortable, breathe deeply and ask God to speak to you. Believe that He will and that He wants to.

- Read the short Bible passage gently and slowly several times. Try to savour each word.
- Reflect on the text of the passage and think about how it could apply to your life right now.
- Respond to the passage by deliberately opening your heart to God.
- Listen to God. What invitation is he making to you?

Here are some comforting verses you could start with:

'He will wipe away every tear from their eyes, and death shall be no more, neither shall there be mourning, nor crying, nor pain anymore, for the former things have passed away.' Revelation 21:4

'The Lord is near to the brokenhearted and saves the crushed in spirit.' Psalm 34:18

'He heals the brokenhearted and binds up their wounds.' Psalm 147:3

'Cast all your anxieties on him, because he cares for you.' 1 Peter 5:7

'To pray is to confess not the abundance but the exhaustion of one's verbal, intellectual and spiritual resources. It is surrender...'

Alan E Lewis[1]

2. Soak in God's presence
Free your diary for a minimum of one hour. Get yourself comfortable, preferably lying down. (If you are tired, you may fall asleep, but doing so in this intentional worship space will be beneficial to your mind, body and soul!)

Put on some worship music. There are many kinds of music deliberately designed for private soaking worship. Some will suit you more than others, so you may need to experiment a bit. I suggest that you don't put on worship music you sing in church as it will distract you. Choose music you are less familiar with, at least at first. Allow yourself to concentrate on relaxing and letting familiar anxieties and feelings subside as you seek to focus on God's goodness, his grace and his holiness.

I have lost myself in worship sessions like this on a regular basis for the last four years and found them to be the most comforting, healing and restoring part of my life with God. I get most of my strength, peace, creativity and inner order from these times alone with God. Often God will say something pertinent to me in the music. Or he will remind me of who I am, or who he is to me at that time, but sometimes there won't be any kind of agenda, or spoken word. I will just know that he is with me. Often this is all I need.

It is also very powerful to soak in God's presence with others. I have occasionally invited a few friends into my little prayer room and just allowed them to be part of my private space for a while. Each time, the presence of God has been very powerful, prophetic words have been released, and our lives have been changed as a result.

I have learnt that I can't ever be truly comforted outside of the presence of God.

3. Stretch your body

Fear and anxiety tend to hijack our bodies. If you are tense, your body will store that stress in many places such as your neck, shoulders, jaw and head. Stretching those places out can help to relieve that pressure. Going for a good walk and getting some fresh air can also change your perspective, loosen stiff joints and get your heart rate going.

In some cases, physio or massage can be useful too. I slept badly for a number of months following my Gran's death and needed physio on my neck to help get rid of the tension there. Any exercise will help maintain emotional health.

4. Take a shower or a bath

Even if you don't need one from a cleanliness point of view, having a shower or bath can help to relax you and shift your mood. Taking care of yourself in this way can relieve anxiety and help you focus on new things.

5. Help others
Reaching out to people in need is actually an amazing tool to help yourself feel better. One of my friends is a social worker who runs a group for people with various problems. One of the lessons she teaches them is the power of being useful and helpful to others. It can really help change your perspective about your own life.

I really enjoy doing little things for others such as offering to babysit, popping a nice card in the post or making them some food. Often this helps me put my own issues to the back of my mind, which can be the best thing to help recharge my spirit.

6. Physical touch
Some of us aren't touchy-feely types and the last thing we think we need is a big hug. But we may be wrong! Touch can release huge emotions in us. Recently at church, I noticed someone who was sitting down, looking anxious. I felt I should go and just put my hand on her shoulder. As I did so, it was like an electric shock happened. She started to shake and, as we began to pray together, something really deep was going on in her. She told me that the release started with that simple touch. The right kind of touch at the right kind of time from the right kind of person can be very healing.

If you know you are wired to need physical touch, you can actually do this for yourself. Even taking a little hand cream and giving yourself a two minute hand massage can feel very relaxing. I can remember doing this recently and just breaking down in tears. I must have needed it!

My daughter wakes up early nearly every day. Her first port of call is our bed. She comes in for a snuggle and spends about ten minutes kissing my face and telling me she loves me. It is one of the most incredible ways to start the day and has been an emotional lifeline to me in the last few months.

7. Healthy food and drink
When we are feeling low it can be really tempting to eat badly. I know this more than anyone. Those scrummy donuts seem so tempting and will definitely give us a sugar rush... but it will not last and we will end up feeling low and even experience mood swings. I am sure you know

that what we eat affects our productivity, brainpower and yes, even our emotions. We can also feel very tired and sluggish after eating certain foods like pasta.

The time of eating can also affect us: I cannot eat after 7pm without suffering in my sleeping patterns or in some way digestively the next day. I just know I have to eat earlier – most often with my children. It appears to be the way I am wired.

In times of anxiety and depression we may also want to reach for a glass of wine or a beer or whatever our favourite tipple might be. But again, we obviously need to keep this in check.

Drinking the right levels of water each day keeps us functioning well, too. It is surprising how often we can mistake hunger for thirst. I recently read Joyce Meyer's book *Look Good Feel Great* and found her take on 'Watering your life' very interesting. She talks about how water isn't just good for hydrating your body, but makes your brain work more effectively, meaning it could even enhance your moods.

8. Surround yourself

Who and what we surround ourselves with is very key in a time of grief. It can be tempting to hold everyone at bay. But it is much healthier to spend time with a small number of people you trust, rather than isolating yourself. For a number of months following Mum's death I didn't feel at all sociable. I didn't want to hold big buffets or arrange dinner parties as I always had before. Jon really struggled with our total lack of social life. One day he commented that we had not had anyone for dinner for five months. I was shocked it had been so long! I was so wrapped up in just coping, that I wasn't thinking about the effect my mental state was having on him and the kids.

The New Year after Mum died, I decided to take a group of 22 people away for a few days. I wanted both a change of scene and to give people the chance to have some relaxing time together. One of my real pleasures in life is catering for large numbers and whilst I knew it would be tiring, I also knew it would be lots of fun. We all had a brilliant time. It was very healing for me to be around interesting and funny people again. I kept thanking them for being there, making me laugh and eating my food!

Being part of a healthy church is an amazing blessing. Going to a small group as well as church on a Sunday, or whenever you meet, can make the difference between grieving well and grieving poorly. Being accountable to people who love you is vital, especially in a season of disappointment, trial or pain.

Our closest friends, Ian and Jen, have walked with us through many years now. At times, alongside my lovely husband Jon, they listened to me railing at them, or at God or at myself and I could see the pain in their faces and their hearts as they heard my angst, anxieties and fears. But they have all closed in on me, loved me and accepted me in spite of my outbursts and lack of hope. They have breathed life and joy into our conversations and refused to allow me not to be challenged in my wrong perceptions. They have been a lifeline to me and I praise God for such lovingly tenacious and earthy people in my world.

During these past few months it has been hard for me to lead a Grow Group (the name our church gives to house groups). At times, I have not wanted to pray or to read God's Word at all. I have been angry and frustrated with God and not wanted to spend time talking to him or leading others towards him. But I made myself carry on, hoping that the discipline of continuing to lead would in itself be a channel of healing. I knew what I thought in my heart and in my head were at odds. I needed to allow myself time to come back into alignment. It came slowly and naturally and it was a huge blessing when it did.

9. Laughter

I once watched an alarming episode of BBC's *Top Gear* where Jeremy Clarkson was, for some obscure reason, in a German 'laughter class.' The teacher was encouraging people in the room to engage in the fakest, loudest kind of laughter they could muster. It seemed to go on for a long time. I was not entirely sure why. It was funny, because it was not funny.

The Bible says that laughter – of the genuine kind – is good for us and brings health to our whole bodies. Proverbs 17:22 says 'A cheerful heart is good medicine, but a crushed spirit dries up the bones.'

There is no doubt that a cheerful spirit uplifts everyone. Laughing actually prolongs life, exercises muscles and lifts our spirits.

Laughter relaxes the whole body. A good, hearty laugh relieves physical tension and stress, leaving your muscles relaxed for up to 45 minutes after.

Laughter boosts the immune system. Laughter decreases stress hormones and increases immune cells and infection-fighting antibodies, thus improving your resistance to disease.

Laughter triggers the release of endorphins, the body's natural feel-good chemicals. Endorphins promote an overall sense of wellbeing and can even temporarily relieve pain.

Laughter protects the heart. Laughter improves the function of blood vessels and increases blood flow, which can help protect you against a heart attack and other cardiovascular problems.

Proverbs 15:13 says, 'A happy heart makes the face cheerful, but heartache crushes the spirit.'

Who or what makes you laugh out loud? I have some friends at church who just have funny bones. I love being with them because they are outrageous, atypical and unusual company. I have cried tears of laughter with them. I can be myself and I know the feeling is abundantly mutual.

If a particular writer or film makes you laugh, seek them out, even in times of grief. Your body and your heart need a break from all the crying and the sorrow. Allow yourself some healthy escapism from the endless solicitor's letters, paperwork, sorting, grief and organisation. Watch 'An Evening with Peter Kay', a recording of the Two Ronnies, or even a funny family movie. Seek out those people who have the gift of humour. Laugh! It is good for you.

God comforts us in many ways. He sends us people, situations and circumstances to help and bless us. But I am learning that sometimes I need to be intentional about self-comfort. I need to look after myself well in order to have enough emotional energy to care for others. Taking time to comfort myself will mean I am nicer to know, more able to bless others and fitter in my mind, body and spirit.

As part of my teacher training degree I did some teaching practice in a small village nursery outside Durham. One day whilst doing the register, a little boy aged three stood up and said, 'Miss. I am sorry I am in a bad mood. Me Mam give us wrong this morning and I've brought it with me.'

I have never forgotten that little boy's understanding. His mother had shouted at him and he felt miserable. He had brought that misery with him. It was extraordinary. He had already learnt that how someone treated him affected how he felt and therefore how he would then go on to treat others. At three!

You are not meant to cuddle children in a nursery setting these days. However he received a very big one from me, and a number of other stunned teachers!

If you are neglecting your own care as you seek to care for someone else that is a ticking time bomb that could go BOOM! at any time.

Take my advice and take care of yourself, letting God and others into your deepest places of need.

MOVING ON

Grief can affect all aspects of our character, our thinking, behaviour, emotions, relationships, and health. Recognising that these are common and necessary reactions to grief can help us. But perhaps on top of that we need to be active in helping ourselves. Perhaps we need to reach out to close friends, join a recovery or prayer group, or ask a pastor or Christian counsellor for some help.

One of the most difficult tasks for anyone who has suffered a loss is adjusting to their new world. The house feels empty, life is strange and the things you once did together can be hard or impossible to do alone.

Often people want to know when it is appropriate and helpful to deal with a loved one's things, make lifestyle changes, or form new relationships. I think everyone is very different in this regard. What may be 'too early' for one person, feels normal and natural to another.

My Dad received some advice this year which he found helpful: not to make any big decisions – like moving house or getting a new job (which at the age of 72, I hoped he wouldn't be tempted to do) – in the 12 months after he had lost Mum. This was wise. Many times, I am sure he felt like moving away and starting again somewhere else... but he may have lived to regret it.

The family advised him not to enter any new relationship from a position of loneliness rather than readiness. We were all very surprised when Dad did find a special person he wanted to get to know better. It was only a few months after Mum had died and felt 'too early' for us as his kids. But when is it too early for someone to be happy and fulfilled? I am not sure that those looking in can ever truly know the answer to that.

Dad told me today that he is getting married again! One year and ten days after Mum died. The person he is marrying is lovely and I have great happiness that he will no longer be alone. However, it has been hard to come to terms with the thought of someone different at Dad's side; someone who is not related to us; someone myself and my brothers do not yet know properly. But I have peace in my heart that this is of God and so will do all I can to support them and the wider family as we move forward and adjust in this time of change.

Before Mum died she made it very clear to Dad that she wanted him to marry again. She said, 'I would see it as the biggest compliment if you did.' I asked what she meant and she smiled and said, 'It would mean he enjoyed it the first time and wanted to do it again!' Sweet Mummy! She also knew of, admired and cared for the person involved. So again, I feel we have her blessing.

Asking God to guide us in these matters of the heart is very important. God will show us his timing and his direction as we seek him. I also think it is very wise to seek the opinions and prayers of those around us who we love and trust. What they say can often be a great blessing and sometimes challenge our perceptions of what is going on.

WHAT JESUS IS TEACHING ME ABOUT LOSS

The best teacher during my time of grief has actually been Jesus himself. He is no stranger to being in pain or feeling disillusioned. Here are some of the things Jesus is helping me to realise again:

1. He will never leave me
There are times in grief where it feels as though God is playing hide and seek. Where he appears to be invisible (if that is not an oxymoron).

I know for myself it felt for months as though God was totally silent, as though he had become somehow muted. It was hard to remember that he was still there. It may have been that He was talking all the time, but I was not in a position to hear or respond. I don't know and I can't go back to check.

It is only now that I sense I am coming through the most painful and worst time of my sadness, that I have started to hear him again properly. I know that he will never leave me because he has made that promise in his word. It does not always feel true, but we must not judge what God is doing on our feelings alone.

My friend shared recently that a mentor she knows asks the following two questions:

Firstly, what is *fact* in this situation?

And secondly, what is *feeling*?

Both are important, but it is vital we don't confuse the two. The fact is that God hasn't left your personal building – how ever silent it appears he is being right now.

2. He wants me to look forward and upward
One of the most beautiful verses that Jesus has highlighted for me in recent days is the one in Luke's account of the resurrection story:

'...suddenly two men in clothes that gleamed like lightning stood beside them. In their fright the women bowed down with their faces to the ground, but the men said to them, 'Why do you look for the living among the dead? He is not here; He has risen!' (Luke 24:4)

This passage came to me in a flash the other day as I was busy doing something else. I suddenly became aware of its truth for me, now.

After my Mum died I spent a long time re-living both happy and sad memories connected to her. Times I had laughed with her, times I had made her angry or caused her to cry. Those emotions weren't really getting me anywhere. Because they were in the past.

In this precious set of verses, Jesus reminded me not to look for something living in something dead. She is risen! She is alive again, in heaven. She is not remembering the time I slammed the door on her, or let her down or took money from her purse without asking. She is not giggling because of the time I smuggled her into a gig I was singing in under my coat. She is not feeling sad because she was insecure about what she looked like and needing my encouragement to tell her she looked nice. She is in glorious, gleaming robes, singing at the top of her voice!

It was a reminder from the very words of Jesus himself to look forward, not back.

3. He feels my pain
Another incredible truth about Jesus is contained in the shortest verse in the Bible. When Jesus came to the home of Mary and Martha after Lazarus had died, he saw their grief. Even though he knew that in just a few minutes he would raise Lazarus from the dead, the Scripture simply says, 'Jesus wept' (John 11:38).

I find it extraordinary that he cried here. He KNEW Lazarus was not going to stay dead for long. So why the tears? Was it for show?

I don't think so. I honestly believe those two words show us Jesus' human and natural response to the sorrow he saw all around him.

Jesus understands your loss even better than you do. Don't think it's more spiritual to hold in your tears – it's very godly to let them out.

4. He guides me

As our Good Shepherd, Jesus leads us safely through 'the valley of the shadow of death' (Psalm 23:4). He doesn't hope we find the way ourselves. He doesn't meet us at the destination. He goes with us.

An old friend of mine once found herself lost in the Indian city of Mumbai. She and her husband were driving around completely and hopelessly off course. They stopped to ask a man for directions. Rather than giving them a list of 'lefts' and 'rights,' he got in the car and directed them to their meeting point himself. This is how Jesus is with us. He will never leave us or abandon us. He journeys alongside us, in every season of the soul.

5. He comforts me and grants lasting peace

The Holy Spirit – also called the Comforter (John 14:26) – can give us the amazing blessing of God's peace, even in the midst of painful suffering. I remember being the one who had to ring and tell my brothers that Mum's cancer was inoperable and she had been given days to live. I was so sad, but I was not stressed. I felt a strange and unnatural sense of peace over me that I couldn't explain.

Philippians 4:6–7 describes this kind of peace for us more: 'Be anxious for nothing, but in everything by prayer and supplication, with thanksgiving, let your requests be made known to God; and the peace of God, which surpasses all understanding, will guard your hearts and minds through Christ Jesus.'

The peace of God is not a passive, tree-hugging 'give peace a chance' flowery kind of peace. It is active and soldier-like, guarding our hearts and our minds, standing at the door and not allowing pain, negativity or fear entrance.

This kind of peace does not come from our circumstances, but from drawing close to Him. It is the kind of peace Andy and Michele describe in Chapter Five.

TALKING TO GOD ABOUT OUR GRIEF

On Wednesday 27ᵗʰ August 2008, the BBC News website reported that "A man who allegedly chose 'Lloyds is pants' as his telephone banking password said he found it had been changed by a member of (Lloyds) staff to 'No it's not.'

Steve Jetley from Shrewsbury said he chose the password after falling out with Lloyds TSB over insurance that came free with an account. He said he was then banned from changing it back or to another password of 'Barclays is better.'

The bank apologised and said the staff member no longer worked there. (I bet it did!)

Mr Jetley said he first realised his security password had been changed when a call centre staff member told him his code word did not match with the one on the computer.

'I thought it was actually quite a funny response,' he said. 'I tried 'Barclays is better' and that didn't go down too well either. But what really incensed me was when I was told I could not change it back to 'Lloyds is pants' because they said it was not appropriate.'

'I asked if it was the word 'pants' they didn't like, and would 'Lloyds is rubbish' do? But they didn't think so. The rules seemed to change, and they told me it had to be one word, so I tried 'censorship', but they didn't like that, and then said it had to be no more than six letters long.'

I found this story rather hilarious!

We are, obviously, a password-rich society. We all need to remember digits, random letters, maiden names and inside leg measurements in order to access current accounts and pay our bills. I hate it when I type in my password and scary red writing appears saying 'Incorrect Username' or some such techno-babble-rubbish. I then have to think again of the many pet names Jon calls me on a regular basis and wonder which one I assigned to this particular cyber-beast.

I actually find the subversive nature of the hero of the adjacent story rather heart-warming. He wanted to open his account by declaring that those running his account were substandard. He exercised his right to free speech, only to be told that his speech was... not so free... and had to be no more than six letters long!

Perhaps he has since had other suggestions made to him by friends and family and potentially even other banks. Who knows.

The truth is that we don't need to work hard to get God's attention when we are grieving, or at any time.

We don't need any kind of access code or password to be heard in heaven. There are no religious patterns or phrases needed that will impress God with our worthiness. In fact, he likes the opposite!

He likes heartfelt simple genuine prayers made by ordinary people exercising free speech. He doesn't even mind if what we say is more than six characters long. He doesn't mind our complaints and our grumblings, our achievements and our failures. None of them will get an 'Incorrect Username' type of response. God always recognises us and accepts us as we are.

He is not afraid of your emotions. He will not judge you for having them and he will not condemn you either. He is the best and most caring listener you could wish for.

So talk to him. Tell him how you feel. Shout at him if you need to.

Question him. Ask him to reveal himself and make himself heard.

His desire is that you know his presence right now.

As I have written this book, I have found it so comforting to know his presence with me. I have prayed for you that you would have found my journey – and the stories of others in times of distress – helpful too.

Looking back over these last few months, I have realised that God has not been walking next to me, or behind me, or ahead of me. He has been carrying me. That has been a deliberate choice on His part and on mine. I have totally let him. Like a small child who has run out of energy on a long walk home, I have opened up my little arms to him. Without words or questions, I have found myself swooped up into his strong everlasting embrace. I cannot think of a safer place. Even grief can be good from such a position.

If you need to make that choice today, perhaps you could pray this short prayer with which I will end my book:

Father God,

Thank you that you know what I need. Thank you that my pain is not hidden from you. Thank you that you have kept all my tears in a bottle and that they are precious to you. I give you my hurts, my pain, my memories, my failure to trust, my insecurities and my questions. I give you myself again right now, just as I am, without pretence. Thank you that I know you can hold my full weight. Please pick me up again and take me where I need to go in this season. Help me learn all you are teaching me. Help me learn it well. Help me to please you, even in these days of my personal grief and pain. Thank you for your comfort and your peace, even in the midst of the storm. I am stronger, braver, wiser and more able in your arms.

Amen.

May God continue to hold you and may you continue to let him. Whatever comes.

With love,

Ems

APPENDIX 1
WHAT TO DO
WHEN SOMONE DIES

'There are stars whose light only reaches the earth long after they have fallen apart. There are people whose remembrance gives light in this world, long after they have passed away. This light shines in our darkest nights on the road we must follow.'

The Talmud

You may have never faced death before, or you may never have been the one who has to organise things when it does happen. This chapter contains all the 'nitty gritty' things I wish I had known when this happened to me.

Remember, God is with you! 'And I will ask the Father, and he will give you another Helper, to be with you forever.' (John 14:16)

PRACTICALITIES

When a person you loved has died, you may feel very shocked, however well prepared you thought you were. You may also feel confused, numb or bewildered. You don't have to rush to do anything. You can just stay with your relative or friend's body for a while.

If you are in a hospital or hospice, the medical staff will be nearby to show you what to do and support you. If your relative died at home, you should let their local GP know within a few hours. The GP or district nurse, or someone who is covering for them, will come as soon as possible in order to verify the death. If you're alone, you may want to ring a relative or friend to come and be with you. If you are part of a church family, you may want to contact an elder or the pastor of your church, too.

After you have verified the death, you will then need a death certificate. This can be given by the doctor who has provided care during the final illness and who has seen the deceased within 14 days of death (28 days in Northern Ireland) or after death. They should be confident about the cause of death. The death certificate is given to the next of kin who is required to deliver it to the Registrar of Births, Deaths and Marriages within five days.

> My flesh and my heart may fail, but God is the strength
> of my heart and my portion forever.
>
> Psalm 73:26

REGISTERING A DEATH

Some registrar's offices have an appointment system, so check before you go. You may be able to book in online. You can find the number of your local registrar's office listed under 'Registration of births, deaths and marriages' online at your local council website. It may also be on the envelope containing the medical certificate.

The registrar will ask you several questions about the person who has died. You need to take the medical certificate, and details of the deceased's place and date of birth, last address, maiden name (or previous names) to the register office in the area where the death occurred. They will then enter the details in a register, which you will need to sign. A certified copy of the entry in the register, commonly known as a 'death certificate', will then be completed.

If you're not able to do this yourself, certain other people can act as an 'informant' and register the death for you. Details of who can act as an informant are listed on the back of the 'Notice to Informant'. These include a relative of the person who has died or a person who is not a relative but who was present at the time of death.

The information you need to provide when registering a death depends on where you live in the UK, so it's important to read the details of the 'Notice to Informant' carefully and make sure you have all the information before you go to the register office. The appointment takes around half an hour. I would recommend taking someone with you.

If the registrar decides that the death does not need reporting to the Coroner he or she will issue:

1. A Certificate for Burial or Cremation (A green form, to say that the death has been registered and that the funeral can take place. You need to give this to the undertaker.
2. A Certificate of Registration of Death Form (BD8) for Social Security purposes
3. (On request), copies of the Death Register
4. If the body is to be buried in England, there are no further formalities. If the burial is to be outside of England, an 'Out of England Order' is needed from the coroner. If the burial is to be at sea, an 'Out of England Order' and a licence from the Ministry of Agriculture, Food and Fisheries is needed, and the District Inspector of Fisheries should be notified.

> Peace I leave with you; my peace I give to you. Not as the world gives do I give to you. Let not your hearts be troubled, neither let them be afraid.
>
> John 14:27 (ESV)

NUMBER OF COPIES

Before you attend the registrar's office, it's helpful to think about how many copies of the death certificate you might need. You can buy 'certified copies' for a small charge at the time of registration. They are duplicate original certified copies of entry, not photocopies. It is wise to obtain the copies you need when you register the death as certificates obtained at a later date will cost quite a bit more.

You will usually need one certified copy for each life insurance policy, or similar, which you need to claim. Other organisations, such as a bank, will just need to see the original certificate or will make a copy for their records. The executor, if there is a will, can help you work out how many copies you will need. (I suggest around five is a good start.)

ARRANGING A FUNERAL

The funeral can usually only take place after the death has been registered. Most people use a funeral director, but you can arrange a funeral yourself. To do this you need to contact the Cemeteries and Crematorium Department of your local council.

Funeral directors and undertakers all provide a 24-hour service so you can ring them at any time. However, you may want to wait until morning if the death has occurred during the night.

They will come and collect the person's body as soon as the death has been verified by a doctor, if this is your wish.

If there is time beforehand, get more than one quote to compare costs. You should choose a funeral director who's a member of either the National Association of Funeral Directors or the Society of Allied and Independent Funeral Directors. Both of these organisations have clear codes of practice and will give you a price list when asked.

Ask local people whom they recommend. In my experience, old family firms who have been working in the profession for years and have a trusted reputation are the best kind. The minute I spoke to our funeral director on the phone after Mum had died, I knew we were in safe hands. The reassurance of that first phone call, the sense of professional calm and yet wonderful care was astounding.

Our home visit by the man who became our personal funeral director was a meeting I will never forget. We sat in a circle, shell-shocked and struggling as David Gresty gently led us through the practicalities. At the hardest time for us as a family, we all knew that we were being taken care of.

FUNERAL COSTS

Funeral costs can include:

1. Funeral director fees which include collecting and looking after the deceased person in a Chapel of Rest, providing staff and cars to and from the church or cemetery.
2. Things the funeral director pays for on your behalf (called 'disbursements') such as a newspaper announcement about the death
3. Local authority burial fees

Often funeral directors list all these costs in their quote.

They should also be able to help you with organising Orders of Service for the cremation or funeral if required. Many can also recommend local catering services for you.

PAYING FOR A FUNERAL

The funeral can be paid for:

1. By you or other family members or friends
2. From a financial scheme the person had – for example, a pre-paid funeral plan or insurance policy
3. From money from the person's estate (their savings). Getting access to this is called applying for a 'grant of representation' (more often called 'applying for probate')

If you have difficulty paying for the funeral, and are on certain benefits you may also be entitled to apply for a funeral payment. See the government website www.gov.uk/after-a-death/overview for more information.

BURIAL OR CREMATION

After the memorial service, the body of the person is cremated or buried.

Cremation takes place in a designated crematorium, which is sometimes close to a church. The ashes of the person are given in a container to the next of kin. You may have discussed with your loved one what they wanted to be done with their ashes and you can carry out these wishes when you are ready.

Burial is usually in a churchyard or other designated burial place. It's also possible for people to be buried in other places, such as a garden. If you want to bury the person on property that you own or in a place that they loved, you can get information from The National Death Centre.

If you and your relative or friend didn't have the chance to discuss their choice of burial or cremation, and there is a will, it's important to consult the executor to see if the will contains this information. If you discussed plans for the funeral before death, this makes it easier to be sure you're arranging a service of remembrance which reflects the person's wishes. Some people also have strong views on the clothes they want to be buried or cremated in.

NOTIFYING ORGANISATIONS

There are a number of organisations who will need to be notified about the death as soon as possible. The 'Tell Us Once' service offered at the time of registering the death will help get the ball rolling.

The most important ones are:

1. The deceased's solicitor
2. HM Revenue & Customs (HMRC) regarding pensions and income
3. National Insurance (NI) contributions office
4. DVLA
5. Passport Office
6. Local council
7. Banks and financial organisations
8. Utility companies

The Money Advice Service offer a complete list of the official organisations and authorities you need to notify in the first weeks following a death and how soon you need to contact them. There are also template letters for you to use when you're contacting everyone. I wish I had known about this site after Mum died. It's so helpful.

Here is some more detailed information about what to send and when:

HM REVENUE & CUSTOMS (HMRC)

You may have to send different forms to HMRC depending on the person's circumstances (for example, income, pensions, benefits, whether there's a surviving spouse or partner).

The HMRC's Bereavement Tool is excellent and can help you work out which forms to fill out and where to send them by filling in a questionnaire. Just click on the link on their site to access it.

NATIONAL INSURANCE (NI) CONTRIBUTIONS OFFICE

You may need to contact the NI contributions office to cancel the deceased's NI payments if they were:

1. self employed
2. making voluntary payments e.g. to make up for a gap in their NI record

HMRC will automatically stop collecting NI if you tell them of the death.

DVLA

You must contact DVLA to:

1. Return any driving licence and cancel the car tax of the deceased
2. Tell them the registration numbers of any vehicles that belonged to the deceased

RETURNING A PASSPORT

If the person had a passport, you should cancel it to prevent it being used illegally. You can return it using a form or simply hand it into your nearest passport office.

YOUR LOCAL COUNCIL

Contact your local council to cancel things like Council Tax and resident parking permits. Councils also offer bereavement services. Talking through your feelings at this time may be helpful. There are many organisations, such as Cruse, which run groups for people who are grieving. Your GP can put you in touch with a local bereavement counsellor if you would like more formal one-to-one counselling.

BANKS AND OTHER FINANCIAL ORGANISATIONS

You may need to close down (or change the details of) the person's bank accounts or financial schemes. This may include contacting their bank, mortgage provider, insurance companies and pension provider.

WILLS AND PROBATE

Probate is the official validation and approval of a will. Application for probate must be made to the local probate court before the will can be executed (carried out). This will take several weeks and can take many months in more complex cases.

If a person dies without making a will this is known as 'dying intestate'. If this is the case, 'letters of administration' should be applied for but this process may take even longer. None of the dead person's property should be sold or given away until probate is granted. If you have questions about probate it might be helpful to discuss these with a solicitor.

In Scotland, probate is called 'confirmation' and 'appointment of executor-dative' is equivalent to 'letters of administration'.

It's important that the executors of the will understand their role and that they keep you up-to-date on progress. If you are a likely beneficiary of the will, bear in mind that probate can take a long time. Try to make sure that you have access to enough money in your own account to see you through the first few weeks and months. Some money can be released early to pay for immediate incidental costs, but it's much easier to have independent funds in a joint account.

Age UK has a brilliant fact sheet about how to deal with someone's estate.

WHEN A DEATH IS REPORTED TO A CORONER

A doctor may report the death to a coroner if:

1. The cause of death is unknown
2. The death was violent or unnatural
3. The death was sudden and unexplained
4. The person who died was not visited by a medical practitioner during their final illness
5. The medical certificate isn't available
6. The person who died wasn't seen by the doctor who signed the medical certificate within 14 days before death or after they died
7. The death occurred during an operation or before the person came out of anaesthetic
8. The medical certificate suggests the death may have been caused by an industrial disease or industrial poisoning

The coroner may decide that the cause of death is clear. In this case:

1. The doctor will sign a medical certificate
2. You take the medical certificate to the registrar
3. The coroner issues a certificate to the registrar stating a post-mortem isn't needed

POST-MORTEMS

To find out how the person died, the coroner may decide a post-mortem is needed. This can be done either in a hospital or mortuary.

You can't object to a coroner's post-mortem, but if you've asked, the coroner must tell you (and the person's GP) when and where the examination will take place.

After the post-mortem:

1. The coroner will release the body for a funeral once they have completed the post-mortem examinations and no further examinations are needed
2. If the body is released with no inquest, the coroner will send a form (known as 'Pink Form - form 100B') to the registrar stating the cause of death
3. If the body is to be cremated, the coroner will also send a 'Certificate of Coroner – form Cremation 6'

If the coroner decides to hold an inquest:

A coroner must hold an inquest if the cause of death is still unknown, or if the person:

1. Possibly died a violent or unnatural death
2. Died in prison or police custody

You can't register the death until after the inquest. The coroner is responsible for sending the relevant paperwork to the registrar.

The death can't be registered until after the inquest, but the coroner can give you a certificate to prove the person is dead. When the inquest is over the coroner will tell the registrar what to put in the register.

There are many people who can help you at this time. I pray that you find them.

APPENDIX 2
USEFUL READING

USEFUL READING

www.muchloved.com/gateway/grief-support-organisations.htm will give you a list of specific charities that may be helpful.

Most of the books that helped me through my grief are about heaven or stories about Christians who have had similar experiences. I have also found the Care for the Family website helpful.

The following link gives a huge number of available resources: http://www.careforthefamily.org.uk/Family+life/bereavement-support/supporting_bereaved_people/helpful_books_bereavement

These include:
* *Infinity and Beyond: A Love Story without End* by Lynette Leitch (Canaan Press)
* *Heaven is for Real: A Little Boy's Astounding Story of His Trip to Heaven and Back* by Todd Burpo (Thomas Nelson)
* *Heaven Is So Real* by Choo Thomas (Charisma House)
* *Flight to Heaven* by Capt Dale Black (Bethany House)
* *The Boy Who Came Back From Heaven* by Kevin Malarkey (Tyndale)
* *God on Mute* by Pete Greig (Kingsway)

GENERAL BEREAVEMENT BOOKS

* *A Grace Disguised* by Jerry Sittser (Zondervan)
* *Living With Bereavement* by Sue Mayfield (Lion)
* *Tracing the Rainbow* by Pablo Martinez and Ali Hull (Authentic)
* *Finding Your Way After the Suicide of Someone You Love* by David Biebel and Suzanne Foster(Zondervan)
* *Inside Grief* by Kathy O'Brien (Printworks)
* *A Special Scar* by Alison Wertheimer (Routledge)

FOR CHILDREN

- *Water Bugs and Dragonflies: Explaining Death to Young Children* by Doris Stickney (Pilgrim Press)
- *Tapestry* by Susie Poole and Bob Hartman (Authentic Media)
- *Heaven is for Real for Kids* by Todd and Sonja Burpo (Thomas Nelson)
- *Badger's Parting Gifts* by Susan Varley (Andersen)

FOR BEREAVED PARENTS

- *Lament for a Son* by Nicholas Wolsterstorff (Eerdmans)
- *The Shaming of the Strong* by Sarah Williams (Regent College Publishing)
- *Always With You* by Gloria Hunniford (Hodder & Stoughton)
- *The Worst Loss* by Barbara D Rosof (Owl Books)
- *The Bereaved Parent* by Harriet Sarnoff Schiff (Souvenir Press)

FOR THOSE WIDOWED YOUNG

- *A Grief Observed* by C S Lewis (Faber)
- *Death and How to Survive It* by Kate Boydell (Ebury)
- *Living With Loss* by Liz McNeill Taylor (Robinson)
- *Widow's Journey* by Xenia Rose (Souvenir Press)
- Surviving Your Partner by Sylvia Murphy (How To Books)
- *Mum's List* by St John Greene (Penguin)

FOR FAMILIES

- Keeping Your Kids Afloat When it Feels Like You're Sinking by Cyndi Lamb Curry (Vine)
- Children and Bereavement by Wendy Duffy (Church House)
- *Straight Talk About Death for Teenagers* by Earl A Grollman (Beacon)
- *Someone Has Died Suddenly* by Mary Williams (Brake)
- *Muddles, Puddles and Sunshine* by Diana Crossley (Hawthorn Press)
- *Beyond the Rough Rock* by Stubbs, Stokes and Baker (Winston's Wish)

ENDNOTES

Preface
1. From *Despicable Me* (film), directed by Pierre Coffin, Chris Renaud. USA: Universal Studios, 2010.
2. John Green, *The Fault In Our Stars*, Penguin, 2013.
3. AMP
4. Sarah Dessen, *The Truth About Forever*, Penguin, 2008.
5. C.S Lewis, *A Grief Observed*, Harper San Francisco, 1963.
6. Lewis Caroll, *Alice's Adventures in Wonderland*, Dover Publications Inc, 1993.

Chapter One
1. Lemony Snicket, *The Bad Beginning (A Series Of Unfortunate Events)*, Egmont Books, 2010.
2. Reported by Arnold Gingrich in *Coronet*, Volume 17 (1944).
3. All blog posts cited are from my personal blog at http://emshancock.com/blog.php
4. Israel Houghton, 'You Hold My World' from album 'Love God. Love People', © 2010 Integrity Music.
5. Keith Getty and Stuart Townend, 'In Christ Alone', © 2001 Thankyou Music.
6. Sarah Ockler, *Twenty Boy Summer*, Little Brown Young Readers, 2010.
7. C.S. Lewis, *A Grief Observed*, Faber and Faber, 2013.
8. Rev David Howell, 'The Armour of God' (pamphlet).

Chapter Two
1. Elisabeth Kubler-Ross, *Death: The Final Stage of Growth*, Prentice Hall, 1975.
2. Isaiah 61:2 NIV.
3. Proverbs 18:24 NIV.
4. Psalm 4:1 NKJV.
5. Luke 22:31-32 NKJV.
6. Bob and Debbie Gass with Ruth Gass Halliday, *The Word for Today*, UCB, 2012.
7. Ann Graham Lotz, *Just Give Me Jesus*, Word Publishing, 2000.

Chapter Three
1. 'Navy Seals Ethos' HYPERLINK "http://www.sealswcc.com/navy-seals-ethos.aspx#.UfGCsRbR3zl" www.sealswcc.com/navy-seals-ethos.aspx#.UfGCsRbR3zl accessed July 2013.
2. Hosea 12:3,4 NIV.
3. Sermon by Rev Bruce Goettsche, October 4, 1999. unionchurch.com/archive/100399.html, accessed July 2013.
4. Jeremiah 29:11 and Ephesians 2:10 NIV.
5. Job 22:28 NKJV.
6. Bob and Debbie Gass with Ruth Gass Halliday, *The Word for Today*, UCB, 2012.
7. Proverbs 18:21 NKJV.
8. Sting, 'I Was Brought To My Senses' © 1996 Steerprice Ltd / Magnetic Publishing Ltd.
9. Proverbs 23:7 NKJV.

Chapter Four
1. ESV.
2. Roy Lawrence, Finding *Hope and Healing through the Bible*, Speedwell Press, 2012.
3. John W James, *The Grief Recovery Handbook*, HarperCollins, 1988.
4. John Stott, *Issues facing Christians Today*, Marshall M&S, 1984.
5. NIV.
6. vv 1-8 NIV.
7. ESV.
8. From Aladdin (film), directed by Ron Clements, John Musker. USA: Walt Disney Pictures, 1992.
9. NIV.
10. AMP.
11. ESV.
12. NIV.
13. NIV.
14. NIV.

Chapter Five

1. Julian Barnes, *Flaubert's Parrot*, Bloomsbury, 1992.
2. Bruce Stanley, *Happiness (Wise Traveller Series)*, Scripture Union, 2007.
3. Many of Andy's words here formed part of the journal that he wrote at the time.
4. Lisa Kleypas, *Sugar Daddy*, Ulverscroft, 2008.
5. Taken from Dennis Wrigley, *From Darkness Into Light*, Maranatha 2010.
6. C.S. Lewis letter dated April, 29 1959, from *Letters of C.S. Lewis*, Geoffrey Bles, 1966.
7. NIV.
8. C.S. Lewis, *Mere Christianity*, Harper One, 2012.

Chapter Six

1. Alana Sheeren speaking at TEDxOjaiWomen, December 2011 (http://tedxtalks.ted.com/video/ TEDxOjaiWomen-Alana-Sheeren-Own accessed July 2013).
2. Matt Redman, 'The Father's Song' © 2000 Thankyou Music.
3. Brennan Manning, *Ruthless Trust*, HarperOne, 2000.
4. NIV.
5. Alana Sheeren, as above.
6. Charlotte Bronte, *Emma*, Everest House, 1981.
7. Bob Dylan: 'Death Is Not The End' © 1983 Columbia Records.

Chapter Seven

1. NIV.
2. Wikipedia, accessed July 2013.
3. Augustine of Hippo, *The City of God* (Translated by Marcus Dods), Book XXI Chapter 8.
4. CS Lewis, *God in the Dock*, Wm. B Eerdmans, 1984.
5. Joel Osteen, *Your Best Life Now*, Hodder and Stoughton, 2008.
6. NKJV.
7. GNT .
8. NLT.

9. NLT.
10. GWT.
11. CS Lewis, *The Problem of Pain*, William Collins, 2012.
12. Oswald Chambers *The Place of Help: God's Provision for our Daily Needs*, Discovery House, 1989.
13. KJV.
14. 2 Timothy 2:11-12 NIV.

Chapter Eight

1. Pete Grieg, *God on Mute: Engaging the Silence of Unanswered Prayer*, Kingsway Publications, 2007.
2. Attributed to Sandra Kring from http:// within-thefire.livejournal.com/1781. html , accessed July 2013.
3. NIV.

Chapter Nine

1. G. Kleiser, *Dictionary of Proverbs*, APH Publishing Corporation, 2005.
2. C.S Lewis, *A Grief Observed*, Harper San Francisco, 1963.
3. In a treatise called *Neetishastra* (His dates are 370-283 BC).
4. ESV.

Chapter Ten

1. Gerard Kelly, *Twitturgies*, Integrity Media Europe, 2011.
2. 2 Corinthians 1:3b-4a NIV.
3. NIV.
4. Bill Hybels, *Courageous Leadership*, Zondervan, 2002.

Chapter Eleven

1. Alan E. Lewis, *Between Cross and Resurrection: A Theology of Holy Saturday* (Eerdmans).